THE PASSION

Eileen Jamie Stapley

ARTHUR H. STOCKWELL LTD.
Elms Court   Ilfracombe   Devon
Established 1898

British Library Cataloguing-in-Publication Data.
A catalogue record for this book is available
from the British Library.

Dedicated to Naomi in her age of innocence

ISBN 0 7223 2891-5

Printed in Great Britain by
Arthur H. Stockwell Ltd.
Elms Court   Ilfracombe
Devon

CONTENTS

CHAPTER ONE

DEPARTURE

It is not possible to leave behind eighteen years, seven months and nine days of one's life as if they had never been. As I boarded the train at Farnham Station on that Wednesday morning of the second of April, 1941, I was leaving behind me the sum total of my childhood, my schooling and the pangs of my first young love affair.

I remember well the clothes I was wearing: a deep purple dress with a green edging which toned in well with the large checks of mauve and green of the coat which I had bought locally as a complete ensemble. My small fibre attaché case was brown and my father had laboured lovingly so that my initials of E.S. were painted on it in black with great precision. I was gauche, naive and a snob, though I was unaware of any of these shortcomings.

It is easy to be clever with hindsight. Looking back I can see how great the sacrifice I had asked of my father six months earlier when I had begun to plague him to "let me go". He had never had a son and I was the youngest of his four daughters. He had already suffered the loss of my mother as she died aged thirty-three and a half years. I was only two years and three months old then and so have no memory of her at all. The death of my eldest sister, Rosalie, in February, 1940, was sudden and dramatic and yet it was to take me many years to fully realise just how shattered my father was, and how deeply this latest tragedy had affected him.

I lived with it myself all that spring and summer, equally shattered, yet resilient enough to bounce back with all the selfishness of youth. By October, as I watched the young men leave to enlist, including the one I had thought I would love eternally, I realised that there was nothing left to keep me in this small town any more.

An old school song seemed so apt at that time I found myself singing or humming it most of my waking hours:

"What's this dull town to me, Robin Adair?
What was't I wished to see, what wished to hear?
For all the joy and mirth made this place Heaven on earth
Now they've all gone from me, Robin Adair."

There were to have been four of us enlisting at the same time; we stood in front of a brick-built letter box let into a wall and two applications were popped in but I kept dithering with mine, first it was nearly in and then I would withdraw it but finally my stepsister made my decision for me by jogging my elbow and in it dropped — she never did enlist herself.

I pointed out to my father that unless he gave me the required permission to enlist I would have to work on munitions which I would loathe. He finally caved in some time after Christmas 1940. But my dad would never forgive me if I did not put on record the happenings of All Fool's Day that year.

The Royal Air Force, in its infinite wisdom, sent for me at a given date in March. As it happened my bodily functions made it impossible for me to comply. I wrote off in great haste, explaining that my enlistment would need to be deferred.

Having solved that problem, I realised I needed some temporary work. I needed the money for my keep and, with the war now well into its second year, everybody was expected to work anyway.

Here I struck really lucky as when I called into the local Registry Office I was sent out immediately bearing a little chit with an address on it. I recognised it as being the home of a family who lived in a very nice house in the area close to Farnham Castle. I stayed there for three weeks, earning two pounds a week — exactly double my previous earnings.

I was very happy. The work was easy and the husband and wife so appreciative of my efforts that I was almost tempted to fall in with their request and give up my plans to enlist. However, I did not succumb and in due course deposited my six pounds in the post office.

On April 1st, I decided to withdraw half of it to buy myself some pyjamas to pack ready for my great day on the morrow. When I mentioned at home that I was going to withdraw three pounds and explained what for, I can picture my father still, standing with raised eyebrows and looking aghast.

"But Eileen, you are going to join the WAAF not buy it!"

I set off with one of my half-sisters and we found just what I was looking for in the very first shop we visited. The shop assistant, my sister and I barely looked up when the shop bell pinged. I sensed someone standing beside me.

"I'll call back later" said a voice, but we paid no heed. It was only when I came to pay for the one pink and one turquoise pair of pyjamas at 29s/11d each, that I realised this woman had walked off with my purse. My precious £3.00 were gone. It was back to the post office for the other three pounds. Naturally, there was no way I could hush an eleven-year-old sister from announcing that my pyjamas had cost me the full six pounds. Luckily, everyone saw the funny side of the situation and dubbed me as being the girl who was joining the WAAF with the most expensive pyjamas. Well, it was April the 1st!

The next morning the pyjamas were in my little brown cheap fibre case and I was being hurtled at great speed towards Waterloo Station. I arrived far too early, but not having the confidence to cope with a taxi, even if one had been available, I set off down the steps and the slight decline, trying desperately to recall all the instructions I had been given.

There was not a soul in sight, but for a solitary policeman who was standing on the kerb watching me. Coming from the very depths of Surrey I doubt if I had ever spoken to a policeman in my life, but I decided to cross over and make quite certain of my direction. That was my first undoing.

I had always been brought up to believe that a policeman's lot was to guard one, direct one or to tell the time if requested.

"Another little girl off to join the WAAFs eh?" said the cheeky young policeman. Yes, I was naive and a little bit scared too, so I did not wait for any further conversation but turned and hurried away as fast as I could.

I walked over Waterloo Bridge and made my way to Kingsway House where the doorman was in deep conversation with what one would term a city gent, with briefcase and rolled umbrella. I decided against making any further enquiries, so I walked past them only to hear him calling after me.

"Where do you think you're going?"

"I'm going to join the WAAFs," I said, in a rather haughty fashion.

"Not in there, you're not" was his reply. "That is the entrance for men."

So began a morning, the events of which were to remain etched on my memory for all time. If I was too early, luckily there were quite a few young women equally so. I sat down beside one of them on the red leather (or maybe it was rexine) seating. A great shyness suddenly swept over me, heightened by the fact that everyone else appeared to be confident and at ease. I did not know then that there is always one who knows everything and speaks with the proverbial "plum in the mouth" accent — and I had got that one.

She started by enquiring where my home was and I told her I lived in Farnham. It was then that I discovered I was an inveterate snob.

"Oh, and where is that?" she asked in a very condescending manner. I found myself avoiding mentioning that it was the next town to Aldershot as I feared that even she would know I was speaking of a garrison town.

"Have you heard of the Hog's Back?" I enquired and before she could reply I added "Well, Guildford is at one end and Farnham the other." If I thought I was off her hook I was sadly mistaken. There were endless questions about my schooling and what type of work I had been offered when I had applied to enlist. These were not so easy to parry. Later she noticed I was fidgeting badly.

"What's the matter with you?" she asked in her arrogant manner. I told her that I needed to pass water badly.

"Don't be stupid," replied Miss Know-It-All. "They will request you to do just that later on and then you won't have any to pass."

I was later to write home and relate all this in a letter. My father was to tell me how he carried it around with him when on night duty as a special constable. He recalled my writing "Oh God! — when they finally handed us the receptacle I was horrified by the smallness of the thing."

I went into one of the cubicles and then began one of those moments when you wish you could die. The water came with a gush and just kept right on coming. Once someone came and shook the curtain and asked if I was ready yet and that only served to make me panic more. I wrote saying "Oh, Dad, I thought I was going to flood the River Thames." In the end I became so desperate that I called out in alarm.

"I don't think this thing is big enough, I'm sure it's going to overflow."

Anyone who has enlisted will remember with clarity the seemingly endless questions, the calling of names and especially the attention paid to one by the medical man. One immediately becomes aware that one's own body appears to be different from the others. Once you have been pronounced fit, there comes the final queuing up to obtain one's service number. How innocent one is, believing that within ten minutes of receiving this number, by which one will be known for the duration, it will forsake one's brain and, like the errant water, will disappear down the drain and be gone forever more.

At school I had excelled in three subjects, known then as Arithmetic, English and Poetry, so I was alive to this latest situation. I noticed that all the numbers being issued that morning began with double fours and that the total number was of six figures. When it was my turn to step forward I suddenly became overly polite and pushed the girl next to me forward. She demurred, saying it was my turn, but by that time she had received her number ending with a three. Only then did I step forward to become 442964. Out of the six figures three were all the same, at the beginning and the end — how could I possibly forget that? I was soon to learn that your number is something never to be forgotten, it is branded on the memory until it becomes more familiar than your name.

We must have eaten, but if we did I don't recall doing so. My next recollection is of going to the post office across the street to send a telegram home. We were permitted not more than ten words at the government's expense so I penned "Passed, posted to Gloucester, writing soon, Love Eileen."

There was to be just one more nightmare occasion on that unforgettable day. We arrived at Paddington Station, still wearing our civvies. We had more or less paired off, when we suddenly realised that we were being counted over and over again. The train was nearly due and there was a sense of panic, not amongst the girls, but those who were despatching us. Later we learned that one of the new recruits, having passed her medical and been duly numbered, had scarpered. She had done a bunk and had already called it a day! I often wondered what happened about her during the years that followed.

It was now well into the afternoon and a heavy mist was beginning to envelop us so we were more than happy when the search for the missing "rookie" was abandoned. We boarded the train and headed for our fortnight's training in Gloucestershire.

It was a very busy fourteen days. On arrival we were told the huts were numbered in such a way that girls in even-numbered huts were allowed out one night and those in huts with odd numbers went out on alternate nights. This was to be quite a disappointment for me. Elsie, also from Farnham, had arrived the previous week and so we were unable to see much of each other because of this rule.

I had walked across some grass, which was strictly against the rules as using paths was a must, and heard a voice calling my name. My immediate reaction was to wonder what terrible fate was in store for me for my misdemeanor. I looked up from washing my "Irons" (cutlery), in a tank filled with disgustingly greasy water, to see Elsie smiling at me.

"I didn't think there could be two coats like yours in the world," she said laughingly.

I cannot recall meeting her again, there or anywhere else, during the whole of the war.

There was one other person I had reason to recall in later years. Feeling lonely one evening, I decided to go alone to the camp cinema. I was standing in the queue when a very tall airman who was standing beside me asked if I would like to sit with him for company. I was nervous, though I sensed he was well-meaning, but he suddenly took the matter into his own hands. He was smartly dressed in his uniform, so was obviously permanent staff. I noticed his collar was clean, but his canvas gym shoes were at odds with the rest of him. Watching my eyes taking stock of him he put his hand into his breast pocket and withdraw a snapshot of himself which he signed with his full name. He offered it to me, with a smile.

"Just call me Lofty, everybody else does," he said. I still have that snapshot and the name of my pleasant, chatty, unsolicited first date as a WAAF. I never saw him again either.

During the few hours which remained for us new recruits to be seen walking around the camp in civilian clothes we were the butt of some hair-raising stories to the extent where I, for one, was dreading our visit to the Stores to be kitted out with uniform. Adversely I longed to look like everybody else. In the event the visit proved to be quite painless for me as I went in at the average height of five feet six inches and so, despite all these prophecies, I was delighted that my uniform fitted me well. My only disappointment being that fate had decreed, even after my belated puberty, that I remained as flat chested as any youth. Later I decided that this was probably more of an asset than a liability. I felt I looked more trim than my well-endowed compatriots when my pockets were filled with odds and ends.

I defy any weatherman to give an accurate description of those fourteen days from 2nd April to 16th April, 1941. To say it was contrary is the only possible assessment. There were days when we would be drilling on the parade ground with sunshine on our backs, yet on the command to "about turn," find our faces stinging with the force of huge hailstones. In the main it was very cold.

Doing physical training (PT) was less hazardous inside the Drill Hall. For the first few sessions, when ordered to strip down to our service issue "navy-blue knickers", we would rush to the furthest corner in the hope of being able to hide behind others to spare our blushes. The drill Corporal was correct when hurrying us up with his shout of "Come along, girls, don't be shy, I've seen it all before and you'll soon learn that you all look very much alike, anyway.''

Nevertheless, on the day we received our various "jabs", and were told how we might be affected, the sun shone with an almost perverse intense heat. Jackets off and with our sleeves rolled up to just above our elbows, we stood outdoors in a crocodile with our hands in the required position on our left hips. We were told that once the inoculations were administered we would be free for the rest of the day. We were also warned that there was every likelihood we would feel very homesick and suffer minor maladies such as headaches.

With a surname beginning with an "S" I often found myself well back in any queue and thus able to gauge any given situation. Even so I was quite unprepared to watch recruits ahead of me faint and fall to the grass verge, some even before the dreaded needle had pierced their skin. It made me feel I was invincible.

Once "jabbed" I found my way to the Mess where cups of tea were available. I remember sitting with several other recruits at a table quite close to the counter. At first we all chattered away with great gusto, but after a while some of the girls became almost hysterical, whilst others were actually weeping loudly and shouting out that they wanted to go home.

I sat watching this spectacle in an almost scoffing fashion and thinking they were behaving thus only because they had been told they might. I think there were only two of us left sitting at the table when, to my utter astonishment, I found myself with my head in my hands and with huge, silent, scalding tears dropping from my eyes through my hands and making large splashes on the table. I vaguely recall two strong pairs of arms supporting me through the Mess door and voices offering me words of comfort. When I awoke I was surprised to be back in the right hut and on my bed. My arm was swollen, very red and painful, but I was more conscious of my very tear-stained face and my sense of feeling foolish over my obvious shallow bravado.

There was much to learn academically, not least the ranks and those whom we were expected to salute when we were wearing headdress. We were told that our WAAF Commanding Officer must at all times be addressed as "Ma'am", the way one would address the Queen. There were endless forms, one to cover every eventuality. The trick appeared to be to learn which colour went with which number. This was when I realised that I possessed an above-average retentive memory.

There were lectures, and gas drill wherein we were taught to memorise the smells of the different gases and their effects. I came across my tiny scrap of paper only recently and smiled when I read that one gas had smelt like pear drops whilst the remainder were far less exotic.

The fourteen days were so packed that they passed with amazing speed. It was soon the afternoon of the 15th April and we were summoned to be in the Postings Office sometime after lunch — known there as dinner. We were asked if we had a preference as to where we would like to be posted, though I must confess we were all very sceptical as to whether any notice was taken of these requests.

I still had a yen for the young man who had left me at home in October, 1940, to enlist six months before me. My geography let me down badly because I knew he was at RAF Cosford but I mistakenly thought it to be in Shropshire instead of Staffordshire. It seemed immaterial that afternoon — I walked out as one of ten recruits allocated to Martlesham Heath in Suffolk.

"The only thing they got right was that, like both Shropshire and Staffordshire, Suffolk was another county beginning with an 'S'," I said cynically.

Until that date Hitler had changed my life only as he had changed all our lives, by thrusting us headlong into war, but in the hours of darkness whilst we were sleeping through our last night at our Training Depot, he was changing the lives of ten "rookie" WAAFs.

I recall breakfast was earlier on the morning of the 16th April. We were due at our bedsides at 08.00 hours for a final kit inspection. Suddenly the buzz which precedes a Tannoy announcement crackled in the hut and all ten of us were astonished to hear our names being called. We were ordered to report again to the Postings Office immediately. As we stood in alphabetical order, I found myself on the end of the line. We were told we may sit. Hitler was becoming far more personal this time. News had been received overnight that Martlesham Heath had suffered such severe bombing that they could not possibly take ten more recruits. The first five girls were instructed as to their new station, then the next four girls were similarly dealt with, leaving just me sitting there all alone with my heart in my broad, black issue shoes. I received a charming smile from the WAAF Officer.

"But you are the lucky one," she said. "You are going to Shropshire after all."

In a very short space of time I was issued with the necessary travel warrant, route form and probably sustenance money.

I had not yet realised my geographical mistake . . .

CHAPTER TWO

OFF TO A FLYING START

I set off with my kit, gas mask and tin helmet on my solitary journey to RAF Flying Training School, Tern Hill, Shropshire. After all the bustle of the past two weeks, this sudden cutting of the umbilical cord was such a traumatic experience that my mind completely blanked out the early stages of my journey. My first awareness came with the realisation that the train had reached and, to my horror, was passing through Cosford.

There was a man standing in the corridor looking out of the train window. He appeared as if he might be exempt by virtue of being a farmer, so I stepped out to join him. I have no memory of him except as the stranger I asked how much further must I travel to reach my destination.

He had a broad dialect which made it difficult for me to catch all he was saying, and my nervousness did not help. Even as a child I had found it difficult to cry, but the lump in my throat was for real when I gathered that I still had about another thirty miles ahead of me. Thirty miles was a very long way to a young girl, who only fifteen days ago had left her home, thinking that a shopping trip to Aldershot was a day's outing. I know he sensed the great tension in me and was trying to find some way of taking my mind off my problem. I was taken aback when he next spoke.

"We shall be passing through Oakengates soon," he said, conversationally. "Did you know it was the birthplace of the jockey, Gordon Richards?"

Poor me, I had never heard of Gordon Richards — but was delighted when time wrought the change and he became Sir Gordon Richards, famous enough for even a cypher, such as I, to remember.

Some transport was awaiting my arrival at Tern Hill Railway Station. It was a short drive, slightly downhill, to the first main gate, which was the entrance to the WAAF Guardroom and Married Quarters in which they were billeted. I booked in and was told that I had been allocated a room, which I would be sharing with another WAAF on the ground floor of house 35.

After the Nissen Huts at the Training Depot I was duly impressed with my new quarters. House 35 was right opposite the Cookhouse, which was to prove to be an added bonus for two reasons. Firstly, not having a skilled trade to offer the RAF, I was told that, as from the following morning, I would be employed there; then on my days off it was handy for meals.

However all this was in the future, firstly I must dump most of my kit on my bed and then make my way to station HQ to report my arrival in the Other Ranks' Orderly Room, which I soon learnt was known as P.3. The Officers' Orderly Room was known as P.2.

I have great cause to remember my first visit to P.3. Due to the vagaries of the April weather, I arrived late afternoon. The sun finally disappeared and a very heavy black frost was forming unseen to the naked eye. HQ was a square building, set about with paths and walls, with brick steps leading down to the main doorway. I began my descent, but lost my footing and suddenly slipped the whole length of the steps, my back bumping on each of them until I found myself sitting in an ungainly position at the bottom. This time I was choking back tears as I made my way along the corridors, looking for the door marked "Orderly Room".

No one had travelled up with me so I was quite surprised to find the Arrivals Clerk was already dealing with another "rookie" WAAF. It never dawned on me till then that personnel were constantly on the move and that she might well have arrived from another RAF Station. I stood behind her, very subdued and in pain, still trying to fight back the tears which were not far away. She was young and attractive and I heard her give her very unusual, and to me, very delightful name and then add her address. A tall male Sergeant was also listening. She stated that her home was in Redruth, in Cornwall.

"How nice for you. That's where all that lovely red soil is, isn't it?" said the Sergeant, engaging her in conversation. None of this did anything to lift my morale, which nose-dived dramatically when I thought of the details I had to offer.

My mind must have wandered for a few seconds. I found myself wondering about the young girl in civilian clothes, working away on the other side of the room, who appeared to be quite adept with her typewriter. Because of the dusk, the light from a naked light bulb shone down on her beautiful red hair. Later I was to learn that she was one of the few civilian clerk/typists employed by the Royal

Air Force in the early days of the war. They worked on a daily basis, going to their respective homes each night. We had only the one and very soon they were all dispensed with as more girls enlisted and were trained to take over these positions.

My musing ceased when I was addressed by the Arrivals Clerk, whose first words astonished me.

"Hello! And what have we here? A spy, or are you just travelling incognito under just the initial 'E'?" he said.

Before I could reply he started reeling off a string of girls' Christian names beginning with the letter "E" — Elsie, Edna, Ena, Enid, Ethel, Eleanor and Elizabeth. On and on he went whilst I just stood there shaking my head and wondering how many more he could think of; it also helped to perk me up. The Sergeant joined in the conversation and I turned to look at him. He was a tall, well-built man with a boyish face which I thought probably belied his years. His skin was slightly pitted and his eyes were blue but very tired looking. He wore a tiepin under his tie which pinned his collar so tightly that it looked as if he might have a death wish to choke himself. Yet there was an air of peace about him as he smiled gently.

"I know what your name is. It's Eileen, isn't it?" he asked.

I admitted that "for my sins" it was. Not wanting to be considered a wet blanket, I added "I'm sorry if I appear to be upset, it's not that I'm unhappy at coming to be on the staff here, it's just that I had a nasty fall when I slipped down HQ steps and bumped my back on each of them."

The girl with whom I shared the room in house 35 was an Irish lassie, one of the few Macs who turned out not to be Scottish. I have no great memory of her, not even what her job was, but she was a happy person who was out most of the time. There must have been some rapport between us for I recall my admiration when she told me that she was going home to Northern Ireland on leave. I would have been no less surprised, untravelled as I still was, if she had told me that she was going to the moon. She sent a card — it was a leg-pull about the English coping with an Irish Jaunting Car — and when I started my "Book of Memories" I wrote beneath it "Mac has a point of view!"

Such was my naivety that I reported to the Cookhouse on my first morning "dressed up to the nines" with a clean, stiff collar and my buttons shining in a blaze of glory. When I opened the door and saw the place was a hive of industry, I realised my mistake immediately and wondered whether I should return to number 35 and come back looking a bit dishevelled, but Sergeant Cook had already spotted me and it was obvious that she was expecting me.

All around me were girls doing various chores, washing dishes, peeling potatoes and scrubbing the floor. To this day I can say with my hand on my heart that I had no control over what took place during the next few weeks. Right from the start I knew that I was being treated differently from the rest. For me it was always the "cleaner tasks" — the nearest I ever got to doing anything manual was sweeping the floor. After several days like this I decided to approach the Sergeant. I thought the other girls must have noticed and maybe even resented my preferential treatment. It only served to bring about an even more bizarre situation.

Head Cook ignored all I attempted to put across. Instead she told me she had a special duty which she wished me to perform. I could hardly believe my ears when she told me that I was to pop back to number 35 and return at 11.15 a.m., every day when I was on duty, looking just how I had looked on the morning of my first arrival. I was to stand at the serving hatch as early dinners started at 11.30 a.m.

The girls entered the Mess at the far end and approached the hatch where I dispensed the dinners according to each girl's likes and dislikes, taking into account the size of the meal requested. I was not even expected to put the food upon the plates. The full plates were passed to me and I just handed them through the hatch. This went on from 11.30 until 2 p.m. and I must admit, in fairness to all the Cookhouse staff, I did not once hear any adverse comment about me. I quickly got to know almost every member of the WAAF Other Ranks' staff by performing this duty.

I was doing my stint one morning when a very young, blonde girl arrived at the hatch.

"Haven't we met somewhere before?" she asked. She was a complete stranger to me and I told her so, but she persisted.

"Well, I was here yesterday doing this job," I offered as an explanation.

"No, I mean, haven't we met in Civvy Street?" I could see she was in earnest. She asked where I lived and when I told her Farnham, in Surrey, she shook her head and still seemed perplexed, so I asked her where she hailed from.

"Chertsey," she replied, and I just burst out laughing. "Have you ever seen a girl riding a cycle round the town, in the direction of St Peter's Hospital? You might know it better as Botley's War Park Hospital."

"Goodness, yes that's right, but I thought that was you and that you had enlisted." I explained that it was my sister, the one closest to me in age. Just before our mother died she was very ill and in order to give my father some relief my aunt had suggested taking my sister to Chertsey. My aunt's own two daughters had already left school and were working and she became so attached to her niece that she finally persuaded my father to let my sister live with her. She never did return to the family fold and it was our aunt's idea that she should take up nursing as her profession.

Ricky, as I grew to know her later, was stunned by the strong family likeness. I remained friendly with her for some months as she shared a room in the house next to mine with another WAAF. When we finally parted she wrote in my autograph book "To my Chertsey Colleague" and signed it Ricky, adding her surname and the date.

Payday was every other Thursday and trestle tables were erected on the green sward outside the Mess end of the Cookhouse. It was now early May and the sun was giving us warm, pleasant days. I cannot remember whether it was my second or third payday — nor did I realise, when I woke that morning, this day was to change my whole life. That afternoon we were all lined up in alphabetical order as usual. As the grass was so dry from the heat of the sun, we were told we could sit down on it until everything was in readiness.

I turned to chat with the WAAF behind me. We both had the same initials, but her surname of Stephens came after mine. She looked very young, not much older than me in fact, so I was astonished to learn that she was married. After a while she confided in me that she was feeling very fed up as she had obtained an SOP (a Sleeping Out Pass) but was still unable to be with her husband overnight, as she had just discovered she was Guardroom Orderly that night.

I have always been a quick thinker, so I asked her who was the Duty Sergeant or Corporal.

"The Sergeant from the Cookhouse," she replied, gloomily.

"Oh, there's no worry then," I confided. "For some reason she seems to have a soft spot for me. After pay parade go and ask her if it's OK if we swop duties. I'll do yours tonight and you can do mine. Not that I know when it's due — I haven't done one yet."

I knew it would work — and it did. I never dreamt that by doing that one small favour my whole life would never be the same again. It was soon after it that I coined the expression that I was VIP; not a Very Important Person but just "Very Incident Prone".

Already I was gaining confidence so that my first stint as Guardroom Orderly held no qualms for me, rather I looked upon it as a relief from the norm and a new experience. At first it was just a case of booking the girls out and checking that each of them had the correct type of pass; the normal Evening Out Pass, a Late Night Pass which covered one until midnight and the occasional Sleeping

Out Pass, which would include the now happy Stephens. It was all pretty mundane stuff and my frequent stints at the Cookhouse hatch helped, as I found it easy to recognise the girls. All this experience, when combined with my quick thinking, even solved a mystery that night.

One of identical twins arrived to do her second night on "Jankers" (punishment for misdemeanour or from having been charged with an offence by an NCO). Sergeant Cook took on a decidedly worried air.

"What on earth shall I give her to do?" she whispered to me.

My quick thinking came to the fore. "Tell her to do the same as she did last night," I whispered back.

This seemed to go down well, for it would be in the Report Book, so Sergeant settled for that. After a while we both noticed that the defaulter was making a thorough search of every cupboard and drawer and when asked what was wrong she asked where the polish was kept.

"It's in the place you put it last night," said Sergeant, but I had tumbled the situation and whispered "We've got the wrong twin, Sergeant," — and we had. Now she was told to start the first of her own two nights of "Jankers" and that her sister would now have a further two to do, instead of one.

I found there was a bonus to being Orderly to the Cookhouse Sergeant. She sent me to collect our suppers and reminded me to tell her Staff who was on duty and to send "Only the best". The best consisted of pieces of cold chicken, ham sandwiches, some very nice cakes and coffee aplenty to wash it all down. I really enjoyed that.

It was about 10.30 p.m. when I noticed the Sergeant was looking slightly ill at ease. I asked if anything was wrong.

"It's just a silly headache," she told me. "I often get one."

"I'll put your bed up in the corner, it's my job anyway," I responded, but she said that much as she would like to rest on her bed, it was impossible because there was still that silly old report to write out. I picked up the Report Book, scanned quickly through it and I told her that I thought I could manage that job, if I just looked back at previous reports I could easily get the drift from them. I did not say this with arrogance, I genuinely wanted Sergeant to have her rest but I also had an innate longing to do anything to dispel the boredom which sets in when the type of person I am has insufficient work to do. So with Sergeant resting on her bed, just resting, I set about my new task and was soon engrossed in it. Once Sergeant remarked that I seemed to be writing a lot, but I kept right at it until the last girl was safely booked in.

Morning brought an early start as I had to find the list of those on early duties and set off round Married Quarters to waken them. They were mainly telephonists and others who did shiftwork. To avoid climbing the stairs to waken those on the upper floors we used a long prop, the kind used to prop up clotheslines. We always rapped the windows loudly so that no one could accuse us of not doing our duty should they happen to oversleep.

Back in the Guardroom I found Sergeant up, washed, dressed in her uniform and looking in the Report Book at my effort of the night before. She remarked on the nice job I had done and didn't I think it best that I finish off by recording the morning's events? I did as she asked, folded her blankets and put her bed back into a cupboard, then left for breakfast and my own bed in house 35.

After Guard Duty, it was the recognised rule that the following day was one free of all duties and parades, so it wasn't long before I was in my bed by the window. With the carefreeness of youth sleep came easily. My last thought was that the heat of the sun through the window would play havoc with my skin and that my nose, always my worst feature, would become reddened and sore. But blessed with such warmth it was easy to fall into unconsciousness, intending when I did waken later in the day to launder my shirts, collars, undies and press my uniform.

How long I slept I know not, only a very short while it seemed, when I heard a timid knocking on the door. There was a notice on the door to the effect that I was on day off after being Guardroom Orderly, so I thought at first that I must have been dreaming. Another knock, louder this time, left me in no doubt.

"Can't you read?" I shouted angrily. "Go away, I'm on legitimate day off." The door opened very slowly and a small, timid WAAF popped her head round.

"Are you Stapley?" she asked.

"Yes," I snapped, "Aircraftwoman/General Duties, Second Class — in other words the lowest rank, the lowest trade and the lowest paid. That's me." And all of it was true.

"I've been sent down from HQ with a message for you. You're to get up immediately and report to the WAAF Commanding Officer straight away," the girl said timidly. My cockiness soon left me and I asked this shy, young girl if she had any idea what all this was about. She quietly shook her head and departed, leaving me totally bewildered.

I searched frantically for a clean collar, wondering all the while why the WAAF Commanding Officer should send for a humble ACH/GD and, if I was on a charge, what on earth I had done to bring her wrath about my ears.

There was an internal approach to HQ from the WAAF Quarters, a small stream was spanned by a few wooden planks, and officially this was the dividing line, for no Airman was allowed beyond this stream without the necessary permit. None of this passed through my mind at the time. I made my way past the NAAFI-cum-Other Ranks' Mess, past the Airmen's Living Quarters and the Sergeants' Mess. For the second time in my life I found myself at "The Holy of Holies". Remembering how I had slipped my way in last time, with the aid of the warm sun and a little more care, I managed to descend the same steps with dignity, but with no less awe than I had felt on that previous visit, which already seemed to be a lifetime ago.

I found the door bearing the legend WAAF Commanding Officer and gave the required knock, remembering that I was wearing my hat and so must give the obligatory salute. My feeling of unease grew when I noticed a young, handsome pilot stretched out along the radiator. I saluted him too, for good measure, after which he took his leave.

I looked my officer full in the face, almost defying her to find any fault with me. Dropping my eyes I saw that the Report Book lay open on her desk revealing my large and very distinctive writing.

I remembered the unwritten law that one must at all times shield anyone with chevrons as they had more to lose than lesser ranks. I stopped myself from blurting out my excuses, that would have been unforgivable, so I looked up again at my WAAF CO.

"Did you write this report, Stapley?" she began. I was only permitted to answer "Yes Ma'am," but nothing was going to stop me from saying my party piece.

"But I can explain . . ." I blundered on, telling her about the Sergeant's headache and that I had actually volunteered my services. Still nothing more was said so I added "I'm very sorry, Ma'am, if my effort at the report is not up to standard and I promise you that I will never do such a thing again."

At last she spoke. The sound of her words startled me after the long silence.

"So you think you are in trouble then?" she said simply and told me to stand at ease. I noticed her eyes and the faint flicker of a smile playing round her mouth.

"I admire your loyalty to Sergeant Cook," she said. "You work in the kitchen for her, don't you?" I nodded and rambled on that I would have done the same thing had it been any other NCO on duty.

"Relax," said the WAAF CO, "I called you to say that whilst

Sergeant Cook is excellent at her job of cooking, she can hardly write much more than her name. She fell on her feet when you exchanged duties with Stephens. You presented her and us with the best report we have seen for many a long day. I normally just read and sign the book and it is returned to the WAAF Guardroom for the next night, but I was impressed with your effort, as you only enlisted a few weeks ago. I decided to show it to the male Sergeant in charge of the Orderly Room. From there he took it to show the Station Adjutant and we all reached the same conclusion. Your talents are being wasted if you continue to work in the Cookhouse. How would you like the chance of becoming a Clerk/General Duties?''

For a while I felt as if I was dreaming all this, that really I was back in my bed under the window on the ground floor of house 35.

"Oh, Ma'am," I said, "there is nothing I'd like more," and because I was still three months away from my nineteenth birthday I added childishly "That would be simply wonderful." She passed the Report Book to me and told me to report to the Sergeant in the Other Ranks' Orderly Room (P.3) next door, who would tell me the rest of the news, after which I was instructed to see that the Report Book was returned to the WAAF Guardroom.

So there I was again, facing the same tall Sergeant, still with his gentle smile and air of peace. He put me at ease straight away.

"Did we cope with the steps safely today, then?" he enquired. "So you want to be a clerk, do you? Well, you appear to have some of the necessary requirements already, but my problem is that I do not have a vacancy for you right now." My heart sank. "But if I send you back now you'll get forgotten and your chance will be lost forever."

"Please Sergeant," I said, "I really don't mind how menial the task is, I'll do anything you ask of me."

The Sergeant told me to report to Central Registry the very next morning where I would spend my days addressing envelopes. They would have to be done by hand as I had never been near a typewriter in my life.

I was filled with a sense of joy and amazement as I mused on how "incident prone" one can get — in just five weeks I was to leave the Cookhouse and work amongst the elitist staff of Headquarters. It was only about seven weeks since I had left my home . . .

CHAPTER THREE

ONE PASSIONATE YEAR . . .

Central Registry was a tiny office, opposite the Adjutant's room. I turned up for my first day as an Under/Training (U/T) Clerk to find there was just one male Corporal working there. He had a typewriter in front of him, but it didn't take me long to realize that typing was not his forte. Well, that was his problem. My job was to address envelopes. Usually they were the small brown ones, but now and again there were larger ones as well.

What I did not realise as I performed this mundane duty was how much my geography was improving. As day followed day I found I could address the mail without continually referring to the address book and I had a fair knowledge of the counties, too. It was not to last. The peacefulness was broken by my tendency to be VIP.

I arrived for work one morning to find the Corporal was absent. I was alone quite some time before Sergeant found time to come down and tell me that I would have to cope on my own for a few days as the Corporal was in Sick Bay with tonsillitis. I assured him I would be OK and told him I would probably set about tidying up the office when I had finished my batch of envelopes. I thought the office was filthy. I asked him if I might have a go on the typewriter if there was any time left.

I was cleaning off the windowsill when I found "THE BOOK". It was amongst piles of faded paper and envelopes, where the sun had tinted everything with a mild scorched look and left a legacy of dead flies and bluebottles. My hands were thick with dust, a feeling which was abhorrent to me, but I pressed on and got the place shipshape before I cleaned off my find. It was a paperback, green top and bottom with a broad white band across the centre. For the life of me I cannot recall the author, only the title which was *One Passionate Year*.

The last book, indeed, the only book of this type I had ever read was when I was about sixteen years old — a book called *The Jade Spider*, which I seem to remember as having been written by Ethel M. Dell. I have searched for a copy of it all through the years, to no avail. I can recall the plot quite clearly; the Irish hero with his flaming red hair aptly called Rory; his courtship with his ladylove — all carried out secretly in a hut in the wooded mountains, where his gift of a brooch in the shape of a jade spider goes missing; all heady stuff for a young girl in those days. *One Passionate Year* looked equally enticing, so I slipped it into my desk drawer to read if and when the chance presented itself.

The following morning Sergeant dropped in to see how I was coping alone. He looked round the office. The windowsill was now denuded of all rubbish and the rest of the place clean and almost bare.

"My, you're a quick worker," he remarked, but I wasn't quick enough when it came to hiding the book. "And what have we here? *One Passionate Year*, eh?" he said, glancing through its pages.

A few days later a member of staff of P.3 was posted. He paid me the compliment of coming to CR to bid me farewell and I asked him if he would sign my autograph book. Sergeant had obviously divulged my secret reading for he wrote in my book "To the possessor of *One Passionate Year*" and signed his name and dated it. Try living for four and a half years with those words written in your autograph book! How many people were to read those immortal words and end up by saying "Ah ha — what's all this then?"

I did not know then that four and a half years lay ahead of me — all of which would be lived with great passion. There was a passion for living, for learning, for meetings and partings, for loving and sorrow, for laughter and for tears. Years that would be lived at great speed and with an ever-changing scenario — yes, they were all passionate years — and my own life was to change again two or three days later.

The Corporal, having recovered from his tonsillitis, was posted overseas. He never came to bid me farewell and it left me wondering if he held me responsible for his posting. I barely had time to digest this new factor, or to wonder whether it would bring further change into my own seemingly unimportant life, when the whole of HQ erupted into a hive of industry. Some white paint became available and it was decided that the Officers' Orderly Room (P.2) should be painted first, because, of course, there were fewer Officers than other ranks. All the staff and equipment had to be moved to one of the upstairs rooms; a light airy one with a dais, originally intended to be used for lectures, or as a dance floor with bandstand for more festive occasions.

Nobody told me anything, I was merely shunted to the far end of P.3. There was little daylight as the windows did not reach as far along as this. It proved to be a case of "Man proposes, God disposes", for hardly had the painting started when several of the staff succumbed to bouts of "gippy" tummy, headaches and sickness. I've always suffered from painter's colic, so I used to make excuses and visit the Signal Section to have a chat with a young Scot U/T Wireless Operator. After a few visits he gave me a photograph of himself in civvies, but he had cut half of it off as it had been taken whilst he was walking in the street with his girlfriend back home. Later, when he got his white flash in his cap he gave me another one of himself dressed in full regalia. Our relationship wasn't anything too serious and soon fizzled out, but under the first photograph I wrote "Andy — before I knew him".

It was soon obvious that many of the staff of P.3 were unable to work because of the effect of the painting, so a few days later we followed P.2 upstairs and joined them in the same large, pleasant room. The staff of P.2 had quickly commandeered the best positions and took up the whole far wall, facing inwards, with the tall windows which overlooked the main gate behind them. I still suffered secretly from my belief that the clerks who worked on Officers' documentation were far superior to those of us who dealt with matters concerning other ranks, enhanced by the fact that we had a few WAAF Corporals who held their rank through their early enlistment. They had lower numbers than the usual six figures as a result. Later, new recruits were given seven-figured numbers all starting with a two, so we prided ourselves then that we not only had one less figure but that we were for a time, until it was discarded, allowed to wear VR on the tops of our sleeves, showing we were Volunteer Reserves.

Our WAAF Corporal sat on the dais next to a male Corporal who worked on postings. Sergeant Little was nearest the door. I presumed this arrangement was because Sergeant Little made seemingly endless trips up and down the stairs to visit the Adjutant, and sometimes, but less often, the Commanding Officer. At last, much to my relief, I was officially allocated a desk; well, it was half of the trestle table used by the Documents' Corporal, facing the door.

It seemed the most natural thing for me to learn to read each day's Personnel Occurrence Reports — known as PORs, and to transfer each item from them onto the documents of the individual concerned. It was not too tedious because there were so many things that could happen and no two reports were ever the same.

My overly retentive memory stored up a lot of information on both male and female Other Ranks and was to make me VIP once again.

I had just finished working on the documents one morning and was looking for something to do.

"Goodness, you are quick," said the Corporal. "I think you had better have a go on that old machine at the end of our table." I put a sheet of foolscap into the old typewriter and began doing as he suggested. I knew that it was the norm to type something like "The quick brown fox jumps over the lazy dogs" and to use all the letters of the alphabet thus, but he made no suggestion as to what I should type. He didn't leave me, we just worked on side by side, until he finally asked me for my typing and I handed him what I had done.

"Where's the rough copy of this?" he asked.

"There is no rough copy," I said, "I just make it up as I go along." I had written a skit, which I still have to this day, on every member of staff in the Orderly Room and entitled it "Ode to P.3". There was just one omission, I was too scared to include the WAAF Corporal, for fear she might put me on a charge. Tom took my typing across to the Sergeant. They nattered about it for a while and he returned without it.

"Is anything wrong?" I asked, feeling slightly scared. "You didn't say I had to type anything specific."

Sergeant took my poem with him on his next trip down to the Adjutant. "The Adjutant would like to see you," he said on his return.

I knocked on the Adjutant's door and was bidden to enter. I was hatless, so no salute was necessary.

The Adjutant looked up and gave me a beaming smile. "You're the young girl we took from the Cookhouse aren't you? Have you any more hidden talents you are going to spring on us?" he asked with a half smile on his lips. I remained silent. "I've just had a good idea," he went on. "There's a Bigwig coming from Group soon who wants to have a blitz on litter round the camp. Is there any chance you could type something along those lines?"

"Well, that's a bit difficult, Sir," I replied. "You see, I can't make it up to order, it just happens when something amuses me or I feel deeply about something. I'll try to see if I can manage something suitable for the occasion, but I don't hold out any great hopes."

Try as I might, I couldn't come up with anything. I was feeling quite desperate when the Adjutant next sent for me.

"Oh, Stapley," he said, "I do hope you haven't spent too much time on the poem about litter I spoke with you about, I'm afraid the visit has been cancelled." What a let off!

CHAPTER FOUR

MY MAC

There followed a period so crammed with events that it is difficult to relate them in chronological order. Indeed, it was forty years later that my recollection was dredged up and I could at last remember my first meeting with "Mac", a gentle, quiet Scot, who came to mean so much to me.

Our meeting was within days of my joining the HQ Staff. I am certain that I did not meet him when he booked in as he was far too reticent to have made a "pass" at a member of the staff. He neither drank nor smoked and was also a non-dancer, so I feel he must have drifted into the Sergeants' Mess on a Dance Night, just for some company. We probably fell into conversation as we both stood on one side of the dance hall. He would have been a few days either side of his twenty-third birthday, so was four years and three months older than me. I still had three months to go to my nineteenth birthday and must have looked what I was, a very young "rookie" WAAF.

His Scottish accent had almost deserted him, leaving him with a lovely soft burr which I found very attractive, but he would sometimes lapse into his native tongue just to amuse. He was very knowledgeable and had a great sense of wit, but he never once behaved towards me other than as a perfect gentleman.

From that night onwards we had eyes only for each other, and each evening he would wait for me outside HQ. My most vivid memory is of seeing him standing by the grass verge which ran alongside the flowerbeds outside HQ surrounded by the masses of roses which bloomed in those small strips of garden all that first spring and summer. Every night he waited, and because we were now all working on the upper floor, he was easily seen. It was very soon accepted that he was my boyfriend.

Sergeant was standing by one of the tall windows one evening, overlooking those steps which I had failed to descend with decorum on my first day.

"Your boyfriend's waiting, Eileen, you might as well go as we won't get any more work out of you today," he said. Sergeant was never hurtful, so he added "Still you work twice as fast as anyone else, anyway."

I ran down the stairs and along the corridor, my one thought being to reach my Mac. Every night we went through the same ritual. Neither of us spoke. Mac would take my hand, give me a warm, gentle smile and then, without even looking around to see if any high-ranking Officer was passing, he would lightly brush my cheek with his lips. It was ages before I learned that our meetings were being watched from those long office windows above and that they were referred to as "the scene from Romeo and Juliet". I didn't tell Mac this. I don't think it would have inhibited him, but I didn't want to miss out, just in case.

He was always early and although I bubbled away about the day's events, he never mentioned his. Perhaps he presumed I knew all about him as I worked on Documentation, but the thought of looking at his personal particulars never entered my head. His honesty, loyalty and soon his affection for me left me with no doubts about him. He approached HQ as if he came from way out at Dispersal but always looked smart and there was no smell of oil or suchlike to indicate that he worked on the aircraft. I knew his five-figure number indicated that he was a "boy entrant" and he was then either a Sergeant or a Flight Sergeant, but I didn't realize he already had seven years' service under his belt, nor where he had spent all those years. What little he did impart left me erroneously for many, many years believing that he was an only child, that his father was deceased and that there was a great affinity between him and his mother.

I cannot recall his ever saying to me "I love you" nor did he show any great passion towards me, yet in the main I believed in his loyalty and even that he regarded me with some affection. His light, tender good-night kiss convinced me that there was not another woman in his life — just his mother and me. I wish now that I had been brought up in a different era, in an age when it would not have been unseemly for me to be more demonstrative towards him. Virgoans are considered to be somewhat "prissy", but I did not know that then.

Although I had no doubt about him, I did feel that perhaps this was all he was ready to offer, with his long service behind him and the difference in our ages. I felt as if I was holding an elusive butterfly in my hands, something beautiful but fragile and so I finally settled for the word "ethereal" as being an apt description of him.

It was only a short time after our first meeting that he went home on leave to his mother in Scotland. I missed him terribly. I was thrilled when he sent me a Mabel Lucy Attwell card depicting a "Portrait of an English Lady — never saying die" but I had misinterpreted its meaning long before he got back. I told myself he was gently chiding me — that it really meant he thought I was chasing after him and wouldn't give up! Yet as soon as he returned I felt OK. He went up again on leave and sent me another M.L.A. card and this one really did make me wonder. The picture depicted two small babies facing each other at the bottom of their respective cots. Underneath were the words "Marriage old chap — it's not a word, it's a SENTENCE". I found this most significant. I was aware by this time that many Scots are laconic and that a postcard equals a letter. They are men of few words and sometimes short on showing the depth of their emotions. I was not yet nineteen and they were a new breed of people to me.

I never wanted to hurt him, so although I longed to ask him why he didn't get the slight defects in both his front teeth repaired, I never did and now I am glad that to this day I can remember everything just the way it was.

CHAPTER FIVE

SERGEANT — MY MENTOR

I passed the Sergeant's desk up on the dais on my way to tea one evening. He asked me to wait till the rest of the Staff had left as he had something he wished to discuss with me. I was puzzled and slightly nervous, but as usual he put me at ease.

"I've no doubt in my mind that you are more than satisfied with your change of job, but I've been wondering how serious you are about remustering to Clerk/GD. You can't go on for all time as you are, after all . . ." He paused, looking thoughtfully at me, "You must weight up the advantages. You will already be aware that you'd be Grade Four and better paid, for a start. I've been giving this matter a lot of thought lately. I wondered whether you'd be willing to give up some of your evenings? I'll do likewise — you can come back here and I'll put you through your paces."

I was immediately conscious of the great compliment he was paying me and I knew I could not turn down this chance. I also sensed, young as I was, that here was a Man who, outside of work, was lonely, or perhaps it would be more correct to say he was a "loner".

We began almost immediately. There was no secrecy about it for I learned later that the Adjutant both knew and approved of the arrangement. Sergeant and I worked hard and fast and I think it fair to say that he gained as much pleasure from teaching me as I did from being taught. He dropped the "Stapley" and reverted to Eileen, but I never referred to him other than as Sergeant, though I knew both of his Christian names well. We rarely spoke on any subject other than what I needed to know to pass my Trade Test.

There was just one evening when we sat back in our chairs and took a well-earned break. For a short while we allowed ourselves a little social chatter. We were actually telling each other, but not in so many words, that we both had backgrounds which had prevented us from showing our true mettle. He had been a "boy entrant" and had come up the hard way, so knowing my Cinderella story of Kitchen to HQ Staff in five weeks, it seemed as if he was determined that I should also be able to use my potential. I learned more about the man than the Sergeant that night and we both knew that I would endeavour to make him proud of my achievements.

The learning was easy enough, the bugbear was the fact that I could not pass the test without the minimum of 25 w.p.m. on the typewriter. It was less than six months since I had first seen a typewriter, let alone use one.

The nights flew by and my meetings with Mac were short and always filled with a sense of urgency. We both knew my evenings with the Sergeant were necessary but equally we hated being apart so much. Where we went to I find it hard to recall — probably the camp cinema on wet nights. Whole evenings with him would pass in just an aura of great happiness. We never went to pubs and missed all the dances, yet a whole spring and summer passed in perfect bliss.

In no time at all, it seemed, the day of the next Trade Test loomed before me. I told Sergeant that I didn't feel nearly ready for it, particularly with regards to the typing test. All the other WAAFs were already Clerk/General Duties and were simply attempting to be upgraded from Grade Two to Grade One, which made me feel all the more uncertain.

"You're quick, intelligent, neat and can spell, so please, if only for my sake, have a shot at it," the Sergeant said encouragingly, when I shared my fears with him. "I suggest you take the whole evening off and don't give a thought to the test," he advised. He walked away smiling and threw his parting words over his shoulder. "I'm sure that will please a certain someone who has not seen as much of you of late as he would have liked."

There was another reason for it being a memorable evening. Previously, Mac had put his finger over my lips if I even mentioned my forthcoming ordeal, but that night he took me completely by surprise. Before he held me close to give me his tender "Good-night" kiss, he put his hand into his breast pocket and drew out the most beautiful studio portrait of himself. It was still light enough for me to read what he had written across his breast pocket "Lots of Love, Mac". I knew at last that he was "wearing his heart on his sleeve for me".

"Oh, Mac, it is simply lovely, when did you have it taken?" I asked, and was astonished when he told me on his twenty-third birthday, 19th May. He was wearing civvies and the striped theme set by his shirt collar was repeated on the "V" neck of his pullover and two more crossed his tie. His quiet jacket set it all off, with just a dark handkerchief with two white spots on, peeping out from his pocket. Only his hair belied his service life as it was in its usually neat and Brylcreemed style.

"Did you . . ." I started to ask.

Reading my thoughts he said, "Yes, the first time I went home, only a few days after we met."

I was choked with emotion. "How do you expect me to concentrate tomorrow now that I have this prized possession?" I asked laughingly.

"Meet me tomorrow night and then we'll both know, won't we?"

I slept with it under my pillow.

How well I recall the day of the Trade Test. Each WAAF had a desk placed well apart from the next one. We did our paperwork first and Sergeant's words kept ringing in my ears "Don't look at the others, just concentrate on the job in hand." All his teaching held me in good stead and we seemed to have covered all that was being asked on the paper. It was when the papers were collected and a typewriter put in front of each of us that my confidence wavered, especially when the girls who had enlisted as shorthand/typists from Civvy Street started off at such cracking rates. Again, I called my Sergeant's words to mind, "You are required to do 25 w.p.m. so don't watch the others, concentrate not on their speeds but on getting your own piece typed without too many errors." Nevertheless, I was really delighted and relieved when the test was over.

I resumed my job in P.3, and no mention was made of the Trade Test, so I took my cue and did not mention it either. A few mornings later I entered HQ and heard a babble coming from one of the unused rooms downstairs. It was in fact the room where I had spent so many hours learning my trade from Sergeant. It was obvious from the moment I entered that the Trade Test results had been posted on the wall. All those who had previously been Grade Two Clerks were now all Grade One, which would mean a slight increase in pay. I was just in time to hear a voice read out the following notice.

"The undermentioned personnel has remustered from Aircrafthand/GD Grade 5 to Clerk/GD Grade 4, and has also obtained the rank of Clerk/GD Grade One."

These words had barely penetrated my brain when I heard another voice.

"Well, what did you expect for Sergeant's pet!" said a WAAF standing by the noticeboard. All the joy of my achievement soon evaporated and tears welled up in my eyes. I felt a hand on my shoulder and turned to find Sergeant standing there. Like me, he was probably remembering all the hours we had slogged to bring about my double promotion.

"You've earned both your Remustering and your new grading. Hadn't you better go upstairs and put them to use?" he said quietly in his gentle voice. I walked away, having tasted my first bout of jealousy, but also learned that such a moment is rare and quickly forgotten like yesterday's news.

Mac had never known that I had worked anywhere other than in HQ, nor was he ever to know, but I did tease him the next evening.

"Don't forget to address me in future as ACW/1," I said, not that it would have made a hap-orth of difference, for Eileen mostly began with an "I" and Stapley remained an eternal enigma where Mac was concerned. He rarely spelt it the same way twice — we pronounced it Stapely (except in Chertsey) so that didn't help much!

Perhaps the word workaholic was not in vogue in 1941, but had it been I feel sure it would have applied to me then and also in all the years ahead of me. I loved not only my work but the whole concept of never needing to be on one's own. We did not have to worry what we had to wear each day and every morning was but the start of another busy day. I say all this because it came as quite a shock when the Sergeant pointed out that it was surely time that I took some leave, a long weekend at least.

"Oh, Sergeant, I couldn't do that. Where or how would I rake up sufficient money to buy a return ticket from Shropshire to Surrey?" I asked.

"Well, we do give Rail Travel Passes every three months or so," he said, "and I feel that a break and change of scenery would do you good after all the extra hours you have put in."

Why we were carrying on this conversation near the long windows, which looked down on the Main Gate and Guardroom, I have not the slightest idea, it being the side of the room where P.2 Staff worked.

I think the Sergeant and I were equally astonished when a long-standing WAAF Corporal butted into our conversation. "I shall be hitchhiking down to the Midlands. I can catch a bus the last six miles to my home from there," she said.

Remembering my inferiority where P.2 Staff was concerned, it did not help that this one had a double-barrelled name. We will call her just B.B. — she was a very pleasant person, well built and easy going.

She made it sound a very simple affair, yet my nerves began to jangle and a thousand questions seemed to be running through my mind. I tried to protest but she was quite adamant.

"I am leaving on Friday morning, Sergeant," she continued. "So if you could see your way to letting Stapley off that early, I can help her get started at least." Had I the least inkling as to what I was letting myself in for, or rather what B.B. was letting me in for, I never would have agreed.

CHAPTER SIX

THE ART OF HITCHHIKING

We were on the main road outside the camp, standing in gorgeous sunshine, on a day in late June. I was immediately puzzled as to why B.B. made no effort at sticking out her thumb as traffic thundered past, until she explained the art of hitchhiking to me. Firstly, never hitch local cars or vans, you can usually tell by names and places of destination whether or not they will be of any use to you. We were there quite some time before she flagged down a huge lorry and I listened as the driver and B.B. came to some decision. It seemed that he was going very close to her home and she could catch a bus from there — so I was thinking, what about me?

"I can't do much for your young mate, I'm afraid, but she's sure to get someone going down to London from there."

I was terrified and had it in mind to turn back, whilst at the same time deciding that I was not going to sit next to the driver. Being well built, B.B. took some time hauling herself aboard and then turned to give me a hand up. I never spoke a word, just looked out at the countryside for most of the journey. How could I guess that on that day and that journey I was going to become more VIP than usual?

In no time at all it seemed the driver was saying "Well, this is as far as I go. I turn off here." B.B. was soon out and on her way, stopping only long enough to call back "I hope you are lucky soon."

I stood on the grass verge by the side of the busy crossroads, with no clues as to where I was and a large lump in my throat. The driver climbed down on his side and warned me not to move, he was coming back.

Only then did I notice that there had been a recent accident and that policemen were still measuring for skid marks. There did not appear to be anything gory in sight. I watched the driver thread his way between the fast moving traffic and start to speak to one of the policemen. He pointed his finger in my direction and more conversation ensued. At last he returned to me.

"You'll be OK kid," he said, "the policeman will help you when he has finished his measuring," and with that he wished me well, gave a cheery wave, turned off right and disappeared.

The minutes waiting seemed like hours and I was beginning to think I had been forgotten. I was taken by surprise when the policeman stood up and faced the London-bound traffic, put up his hand and waved down an enormous black police car. He spoke with the driver and then came across to me. I could have hugged and even kissed him when he said, "This is the car I have been waiting for. It travels to Whitehall every day, come with me." We went across the busy road and I recall his next words to this day, "There's the Police Force, the Army — jump in the Air Force."

Next to the police driver sat a young private soldier, obviously as lucky as I, as he too was travelling almost all the way down to London. It was very hot in the car on that far-off June day. The first thing I did was remove my cap and place it beside me on the back seat.

"Been waiting long?" the soldier asked, but before I could reply he offered cigarettes all round. I had never smoked before enlisting but had joined the brigade of those who think they must do whatever is the fashion, so I took one and sat back to relax.

I would not learn until the next day that I was causing total commotion on the A5. My luck held as, after we had dropped the soldier off, the police driver said "It will only take me a few minutes to run you round to Waterloo Station," which he did. I caught a train to Farnham and had sufficient money for my return fare all the way back.

Waterloo Station was far busier than it had been on my arrival in early April. I was doing my best to cope with the milling crowds when I was approached by a soldier who enquired of me, in a very marked Canadian accent, if I knew where he could catch a train to Aldershot. It was now nearly three months since I had left my home and though this time had wrought great changes in me, the changes were insufficient for me to cope with a foreign soldier. More out of nervousness than anything else, and knowing he would be catching the same train as me, I spoke edgily.

"Just follow the crowd and you'll find your way," I said.

One's first trip home in uniform creates quite a stir. On the Saturday morning I suggested taking my two half-sisters into Farnham town. I had no sweet coupons, so I offered to buy each of us an ice cream. I explained that we must eat them in Woolworth's as there was a rule forbidding me to eat anything in the street when in uniform. We were licking away at them when I suddenly felt a hand on my shoulder. I spun round and found my "Old Flame" standing next to me.

"I told Mum I'd find you somewhere in the town," he grinned. "She said not to be so foolish. There are thousands of girls in the WAAFs now and you all look much alike."

"What are you talking about?" I asked, laughing with pleasure at seeing him again.

"It *was* you in a big black police car coming down the A5 yesterday, wasn't it? We were in the back of a station truck cadging a lift down from Cosford. I couldn't believe my eyes — there you sat with your cap off, smoking a cigarette. I must admit the latter threw me a bit. I asked Mum to guess who I'd seen, but when I added you were smoking she said 'There you are then, Eileen has never smoked a cigarette in her life.' I reminded her how often and how close I had been to your face — as if I could forget that!" He went on, "I shouted out 'That's my girlfriend in the back of that big black police car' and we all made a hell of a din. We were banging on the tailboard and shouting 'Eileen, Eileen,' but, of course, you soon overtook and passed by in grand style."

I felt these comments made up for my feeling of inadequacy at being caught licking an ice cream. It was difficult to carry on any conversation with my two young half-sisters "all ears" standing agog. I wanted to correct his claim and say "Surely you mean ex-girlfriend" but eighteen months in (and often out, as far as he was concerned) of each other's company, made us aware of what we should say and what was best left unsaid.

He was going to his present girlfriend's home for tea on Sunday, but was excited by the fact that we would be able to travel together for the greater part of our return journeys. He thought it better if we met at the bottom of the hill. Same old flame, same old arrangements, yet I still found myself slightly stirred as of old at the thought of being in his company for quite a few hours. That was not the only time I was VIP that weekend for another surprise lay in store for me.

On Saturday nights many of the local girls were picked up by truck and taken to an Army dance. My stepmother suggested I go with them but my stepsister wasn't all that taken with the idea. It did in fact nearly fall through for quite a different reason. In those few weeks away from home I had put on weight because the camp food was much stodgier and my one suitable dress barely fitted me. I did end up by going, though I found myself something of a wallflower, because most of the other girls went every week and it was all very familiar to them, but it was not a very pleasant position for me to be in.

I was buying myself a lemonade at the bar when to my astonishment and eternal shame I found a soldier standing beside me.

"Just follow the crowd and you'll find the way," he mimicked.

"How on earth did you recognise me? Last night I was in uniform and now I'm in civvies?" I asked in a puzzled voice.

"You have beautiful hair when it's let down. May I buy you a Coke?" he asked, ignoring my question.

"A Coke? What's a Coke? You're not trying to get me tipsy are you?" I said laughingly.

"You must have led a very sheltered existence on that camp of yours if you've never heard of a Coke."

We spent the whole evening dancing every dance together and he made me promise not to be so apprehensive about Canadians. Later I was to meet Yankees, Aussies and New Zealanders and take them all in my stride. We parted after our one unexpected night together as I had to return on the truck — it was a short but very pleasant interlude.

For all the care my old flame had taken over our meeting the next evening for our return journeys, it was to no avail. His charm and impeccable manners had always attracted me and when he took my case from me, he was not in the least concerned that my initials E.S. could be read, that had never been his style. Word soon got back about our being seen walking towards the railway station together and in time it put paid to his latest affair. Being away from our respective camps made us both feel that the old attraction was still there, especially on such a long journey.

"I suppose if the war hadn't come," he suggested, "I would have ended up marrying you. No matter how often I left you, you always drew me back like a magnet."

"Haven't you got something wrong?" I asked. "Surely you mean you would have asked me if I would like to marry you!" We both knew I would not have made such a riposte in the old carefree days of 1939.

"You are growing up very quickly," he laughed.

CHAPTER SEVEN

THE SHROPSHIRE LASS

Mac was away when I got back and I missed him terribly. Writing was not his forte, so there was no letter from him awaiting my return. Although I was now working on documentation, I had never thought to look up his personal details. There were times when I thought he teased me because it was his way of hiding his true feelings for me, such are the agonies of youth!

He had signed his portrait "Lots of Love, Mac", but I reasoned that many people signed things "with love". I could not forget what he had written on the back of one of the two postcards "If you have anything for me, forget it — as I'm quite happy where I am!" My youthful inexperience left me with doubts about him until he returned and we fell back into our familiar lifestyle. Then I would wonder why I allowed these moments of doubt to creep in and make myself suffer.

Yet even when I asked him to sign my autograph book he chose to write from the Rubaiyat of Omar Khayyam:

"The moving finger writes and, having writ, moves on,
Nor all they piety nor wit shall lure it back to cancel half a line,
Nor all thy tears wash out a single line of it."

What I didn't notice at that time was that when he signed beneath the quote he did not sign it Mac, as he did everything else, but used his initial "J" for his forename followed by his surname in full.

It was later that year and the nights grew dark early; the summer had passed and the roses no longer bloomed in those small strips of garden outside HQ. I was passing my billet one evening and heard the sound of sobbing. Some time back I had moved from number 35 to number 36, though for the life of me I cannot remember why. The sobbing came from number 35. I popped my head round the door.

"Do you need any help?" I called out. Stooping before the grate was a very small WAAF trying to light a fire but having no success because the wood was very damp. We never stood on ceremony in our kind of life and so we were soon tackling the job together. In the process of getting the blaze going we scorched the floor in front of the fireplace. We were both worried at first, but it was no good, I had always been a bit of a giggler and tonight was no exception.

"Let's put the mat over the scorch mark," I chuckled. So began my friendship with Joy.

She was five or six years older than me but because of her lack of inches I seemed most times to be the driving force in the relationship. I soon learned a lot about her. She had been a shorthand/typist before the war and worked in the typing pool in HQ on the ground floor next door to the Station Padre.

Her home was in Maidstone, Kent, not far from the prison, and it was not very long before she invited me home for occasional weekends. On the Saturdays when we were down there, her mother would take us to a smashing little coffee shop where we would have the most delicious cream cakes. "Smashing" was the in word in those days, well, one of them for we often used "wizard" too.

Another vivid memory I have of those happy days is of the bracelets her mother bought, one for each of us. On one side we had our Christian names and on the other our WAAF details, such as surname and number. Her mother, ever hopeful, suggested we omit our rank in case we were promoted! Our next rank would be the first visible one, as Leading Aircraftwomen wore propellers on their sleeves. I suppose one could compare this rank to that of Lance Corporal in the Army, but although it brought some satisfaction, I never felt the rank had quite the same clout.

It was on a damp, misty morning in November when I realised just how naive I still was. We were instructed to parade outside the NAAFI, much to our chagrin, to reacquaint ourselves with the different gases, their smells and effects. I still have my small slip of paper to this day and notice one of them smelt like pear drops, whilst others were far less exotic, one smelling like rotting vegetables. We had been ordered to "Dress" from the right on that occasion, so that at my average height I found myself about halfway along the line. I cannot remember whether we were allowed to partake of breakfast or whether it was thought it might cause sickness.

There was quite a delay and it was very cold. We knew what we had to do; don our gas masks, pass through the small hut which had been hastily erected in the far corner, lift our mask very slightly as we walked through it, then tell the NCO what we thought each gas was. But still we stood and nothing happened so we had begun moaning and were restive.

Suddenly we were surprised to hear some commotion at the head of the line. It was obvious to us all, as we peeped out to see what was happening, that one of the WAAFs had fainted.

"Well, what can they expect? First they choose one of the worst mornings ever and then have the gall to keep us standing about," I said in all innocence to the WAAF next to me.

"How green can you be — and you work in HQ too! You must surely be about the only WAAF on this parade who doesn't know the girl's pregnant!" This was the first of several cases I learnt about in the years ahead. More importantly, other medical matters suddenly became clear to me. Some WAAFs came in and rushed to have scalding baths, jump off tables, swig neat gin, which was referred to as 'Mother's Ruin', and all for fear of unwanted pregnancies. But on that November morning, well, yes, I was still very naive!

It was just before Christmas that I decided to hitchhike alone to see the shops in Shrewsbury. My pay would only stretch to bus fares, some window shopping and a light snack. Even this small trip made me VIP once again. I was standing at the crossroads waiting for the bus to arrive from Market Drayton when a lady driver drew up beside me and asked if I was going to Shrewsbury and if so, would I like a lift? I was a little anxious.

"I am an Army Officer's wife," she explained, "but I do get lonely when he is away. I would enjoy having your company." I was won over and we were soon on our way and chatting like old friends. She commented on the sad condition of the small, blue car in which we were travelling. Time passed quickly and we soon drew into a car park, both noticing that it was market day. I became anxious again when she asked me where I intended to eat.

"Well, I won't have too much time," I said hurriedly, "as I hear 'The Dingle' is beautiful and not to be missed." My latter statement was true, but I think she sensed that I was thinking about my rookie's pay.

"If you would care to join me for lunch," she invited, "I will be waiting for you at 13.00 hours in the restaurant above Boots the Chemists. My treat, of course."

How could I refuse her offer?

Suddenly she changed the arrangements. "Perhaps it would be better to meet back here in case one of us is late," she said as we were getting out of the car. I pointed out that she had not locked her car doors, but she just laughed. "No one would want to pinch this old banger, so if you're back first, sit inside and keep warm," she said. I took the precaution of counting the cars. Hers was the fifth from the entrance which we had just used and, of course, I knew that it was blue, so we parted to go our separate ways.

Who can see "The Dingle" without falling in love with its beauty? Even in wartime it was being well cared for, though I was to return many years later when it was even more lovely. The restaurant above Boots had disappeared by then.

My day out proved to be a memorable, happy one, marred only by my error when I hove up, counted the cars, and finding the driver had not yet returned, I decided to sit inside on the back seat. To my mind it was purely a mark of respect, but that small incident proved to be my undoing. Oh, I have laughed about it often and it was the type of occasion that made me, at a later date, write a poem about it, entitled "Ode to a Rookie WAAF".

I sat in the car for some while and was totally taken aback as the front door on the driver's side opened and a huge man got in. It was obvious from his aroma that he was a farmer. He didn't look round but was about to let in the clutch and depart. My heart started thumping and I even had the wild idea that this was a planned kidnapping. What to do? I decided to cough and he spun round with surprise written all over his face.

"Who the devil are you?" he asked. I started to explain but my story sounded a bit tame and it was obvious that he was far from being in good humour. We both got out of the car. To my surprise he took hold of my greatcoat collar and started crossing the car park with me in his grip. He didn't see the funny side of it at all, just hauled me up to another blue car on the opposite side, where my new friend was anxiously waiting for me.

"Oh, I thought perhaps you had changed your mind" she said, puzzled by the way of my arrival. It seems I had come through a different entrance and by sheer misfortune there was a blue car fifth down on the right there too. I was a bit shaken and she was very concerned but it was not too long before we were enjoying a very good, hot luncheon and having a good laugh about it all.

She drove me back to the crossroads and as she departed she smiled. "Well, I won't forget this day in a hurry!" she said.

There were many trips I made with Joy which I will mention later, but our first Christmas came and we each received a formal invitation from the Commanding Officer to attend Christmas luncheon in the NAAFI, to be followed by a dance. This was for all Other Ranks up to the rank of Corporal.

As there was to be a similar occasion in the Sergeants' Mess on another evening, by invitation only, I discovered that the Christmas dances in nearby Market Drayton were held much earlier to ensure a good attendance. I had occasionally been to some of the weekly dances held there, but not very often because of Mac being a non-dancer.

I have no recollection of my nineteenth birthday, for I was to learn that birthdays had no particular significance to Mac, neither his nor mine. Later that would include my twenty-first, one's "Coming of Age" in those days — but that date and occasion was still well in the future and much was to happen to each of us before that August — in both senses — day arrived.

Someone with artistic leanings had cleverly etched a poster on white paper using both red and green inks proclaiming "Happy Christmas and a Prosperous New Year to you all. From the staff of P.3." I cadged it off Sergeant after twelfth night.

Before enlisting I had not heard that Scots celebrate New Year as being Hogmanay, but I was well aware of this fact when Mac went to his home on an extended Christmas/Hogmanay leave and I attended the luncheon in the NAAFI alone. I kept the menu in addition to the poster. But there was to be a third keepsake for me that Christmas.

I was one of the lucky ones to be invited to the Sergeants' Mess Dinner/Dance. With Mac away I found myself inundated with invitations from other men wishing to escort me. I did not kid myself about this because I was of the firm belief that all members of the HQ Staff were considered as being the elite. I was sent downstairs on a routine errand to the Station Warrant Officer's Office. To most people he was an awesome character, so it was surprising that he asked me, a mere "rookie" WAAF, in a friendly, chatty way, if I was fixed up.

"Well, yes, I am," I said, "but I do have a problem. I've had so many offers and I want to attend, but don't wish to hurt anybody's feelings."

"Well, I'll fix that for you in a jiffy," he said as he opened his desk drawer and withdrew an invitation. I well recall my surprise and everyone's disbelief on seeing that an ACW/1 had been invited by the Station Warrant Officer. I kept that invitation too. I knew he had no intention of escorting me, but I recall turning to him as I was leaving his office with the invitation in my hand and commenting "Oh, you have the same surname as my late mother, only spelt differently." From that day on we became the best of pals.

CHAPTER EIGHT

STANLEY

January, 1942, came in with really thick snow, so that the new course of trainee pilots remained grounded. We were a Flying Training School where each course came for a period of eight weeks and then passed on. Working in HQ, I rarely came into contact with Aircrew, though in time we too were in demand. Each course had an "Arrivals" party, and a "Farewell" one at the end of the period, so it seemed we were quite often a bit squiffy. In my case on gin and limes!

The whole camp seemed to be wrapped in a white world of silence. I had a very bad cold and was looking forward to a night in and going early to my bed. Joy had other ideas. It was one of those rare occasions when she took the initiative and would not stop pestering me to go with her to "Smokey Joe's" Transport Cafe. Try as I might to get her to change her mind and go to the NAAFI on camp instead, she would not budge. It was not the fact that it was "Smokey Joe's" that put me off, for the food and coffee served there were really good for the type of place it was. The long walk, up a dark road with no pavements, did not appeal on such a night as this. I did not feel the need for male company as much as Joy seemed to, being so much older than me.

When I realised I was going to lose this battle, I got ready and we set off. The further we trudged the more mad I thought the whole idea to be. We passed "The Stormy Petrel" on our left on the other side of the road; it was out of bounds to other ranks but I felt that even the Officers and Flying Staff would more likely be in their respective Messes on a night such as this.

On we trudged. The road was edged with hedges and deep ditches, presumably for the water to drain off the land, but we could see none of this. At last a faint glimmer of light came into view. Perhaps, with such terrible weather, the blackout enforcement was being overlooked. When we finally reached the cafe the strong wind forced us through the door and the snow blew in with us. The place, except for the owner, was empty, which did nothing to improve my unusual ill-humour. We sat down at a table far away from the door. At least the coffee was good as usual so we sat drinking it.

I pulled out my nail file and, through sheer boredom, did something really alien to my nature. I began to scratch on the already badly scored table. I was thus occupied when the door opened again, letting in a further gust of snow and wind. We looked up to see two trainee pilots come in. They asked politely if they might join us and we were only too pleased to have their company. Stanley sat next to me and the other chap, Don, started chatting to Joy. I continued etching away on the table — a heart pierced through with an arrow. It was suggested the four of us return and go to the camp cinema but I pointed out that I really did have a terrible cold and would much rather return to my Billet and go to bed. I said it as if I meant it!

Joy and I set off and now it was her turn for a "moody". I didn't help matters much when the subject of her birthday cropped up as being 14th July.

"Oh! The famous date of the Siege of the Bastille," I said.

"Aren't you going a bit far adding French history? Your memory for English dates is more than sufficient," she muttered.

We thought we were alone as we plodded back towards the camp, with the snow now on our backs. As usual I walked on the outside of her as we chatted, silently followed, though we did not know it, by the two trainee pilots, who had decided to head back and go to the camp cinema.

Then it happened — one moment I was trudging along talking to Joy and the next I found myself lifted by a pair of strong arms and I was thrown violently into the ditch full of snow by the roadside. How often I was to wonder if my life would have ended that night if those two young men had not decided to leave the cafe so soon after us. Just supposing Stanley had not noticed that a lorry was travelling ever closer toward me because the driver's windscreen was so covered in snow that he was totally blinded and about to kill me.

The driver never stopped and totally bewildered I was hauled from the ditch and Stanley was saying "I'm terribly sorry, I don't make a habit of throwing young WAAFs into ditches." We were all a bit shaky and I now had a soaking wet uniform as well as my bad cold.

Stanley was very tall, well over six feet, and I clung to him to regain my confidence before my wits returned sufficiently to say to him "Thank you for saving my life."

I think he thought it best to joke lightly. "My pleasure," he said simply.

Suddenly I made up my mind. "I can hardly refuse to go to the cinema after all that,"I said lightly. "I'll play the martyr and go with a cold and soaking wet clothes." So that was my first meeting with Stanley.

Joy and Don were nowhere to be found after the film, which did not surprise me in the least. I suggested to Stanley that we took the short way along the path by the tiny stream, where those planks we used as a small bridge made the internal dividing line between the quarters. I could tell this route was new to Stanley and we stood for a while both conscious of my wretched state. He held out his hands to me, both for warmth and as his way of saying "Good night" to me.

It was then that I noticed the state of his gloves. "Good gracious, what a state your gloves are in, more holes than gloves. Give them to me and I'll darn them for you. I often do little jobs for the boys in the office, like collars and buttons."

"Lucky fellows," he said, but demurred until I insisted.

Situations like this always brought about another problem, so I added quickly "I'll drop them in the Sergeants' Mess for you in the morning, on my way to HQ. I could put your name on them." It was dark but I sensed he was smiling.

"I see," he said. "Is that your way of telling me that you are not sufficiently interested to want to see me again?"

"No — I'm just a WAAF who waits to be dated in the old-fashioned way," I replied.

"So, couldn't you be old-fashioned tomorrow night and meet me here with the gloves? I promise I won't throw you into another ditch."

So began my friendship with Stanley, which I then believed would be terminated at the end of February when his Flying Training period came to an end. But from the moment I darned the fingers of his gloves I was unknowingly changing the course of our futures and those of other people too.

As far as I recall Stanley was a member of Course 66. I soon discovered about the parties each course held but the heavy snowfall had put off any idea of parties so early in this new year of 1942. Mac was still away on his Christmas/Hogmanay leave.

No two men are alike — Mac was of average height, around five feet eight or nine, whilst Stanley was not only tall but of very slight build. I always called Stanley my gentle "Gentleman" — he was an intellectual but when his blue/grey eyes were not in grave repose, he had a lovely smile and, like Mac, a great wit.

I was unaware that I was going to learn more about Stanley after his eight weeks at Tern Hill had ended. Once Mac was back I was happy with him as my companion — he had such a gentle and lovable disposition, but I did learn that Stanley was much nearer to me in age. I was nineteen the previous August and he was twenty the previous September, making just eleven months difference in our ages.

He spoke of Thame Grammar School, whilst I continued to remain silent about the fact that I had not always worked in HQ. My silence made people assume that I worked there purely on the merit of my prewar trade — so I must still have been an inveterate snob in early 1942. The idea that I had been clever in my achievements never entered my head as being commendable.

When Stanley left with the departure of Course 66 I asked the lads to sign my autograph book. Stanley, this great scholar, recalled our first meeting when he found me using my nail file to scratch a heart on the cafe table. He made a real gaffe by writing and spelling thus: "To one who 'scractches' hearts on tables — let this be a lesson to you!" He signed it Stanley, Tern Hill, 1942. Above this he drew a large heart, well and truly cracked and pierced through with an arrow. How precious these small funny blunders become with time — I would not have wished it any other way.

I was still working in P.3 and sharing Corporal Tom's trestle table which faced the door. I cannot remember the date when I first gazed upon a celebrity, though I can recall with great clarity what happened. Being an Officer he was signing in across the room in the P.2 Section.

Tom nudged me. "Look toward P.2 and see if you can recognise the Officer signing in," he whispered.

Since the Officer had his back towards me I wasn't impressed but as he turned to walk out of the large room he happened to glance back towards our desk and I got a very good view of his oh! so very handsome face. I recognised him as being the actor John Justin.

"I think I saw him not long ago in 'The Thief of Baghdad'," I whispered to Tom. He had, of course, booked in under his true name, as I was to learn, but not for many months to come.

Whenever Mac was away he seemed to be gone forever but once back he was all mine again, loving, patient, gentle and forever teasing me. I know he felt the difference in our ages more than I. I was growing into a woman, but whilst Mac could accept my rapid change of rank, he appeared unable to accept me as being other than a young girl.

Stanley was now far away flying his Lancaster bombers but still took time out to pen me the occasional newsy letter, which after such a brief acquaintanceship, both surprised me and brought me happiness.

The weather was still very cold and Stanley took some leave and went to his home in a pretty little village about eight miles outside of Oxford.

His mother doted on him, not without good reason, and he had one small sister who was sixteen years his junior and therefore fifteen years younger than me. This is the story of what happened during that leave — the way I heard it.

His mother, Olive, was tipping his soiled washing out of his kitbag and, coming across the neatly-darned gloves called him indoors.

"Whoever darned your gloves?" she enquired. "That's a woman's touch if ever I saw one." Olive was a romantic, as I was soon to learn. My next letter from Stanley conveyed the fact that his mother had decided that any girl who had taken the trouble to mend her son's gloves so beautifully must surely be worth knowing and that she would very much like to meet me. Even when she was told that we were no longer on the same station nothing would budge her from her desire. I don't think we ever dared to tell her that Stanley had almost certainly saved my life.

In view of what happened I think I must have been in Surrey on a full week's leave; anyway I promised to go up for a day. Firstly I decided to try to reach the sister of mine who was nursing in Chertsey. I still regarded myself as something of a cypher, so was unprepared for the welcome I received from the Matron — she thought it was really great having two sisters serving in different uniforms, each helping the war effort in different ways. I had called on my aunt first but her husband, our Uncle Tom, had only recently passed away and she was still in deep mourning, but she did lend me her sit-up-and-beg cycle and I arrived at the hospital on that. My sister was given some time off to take me to her room where, to my surprise, we were brought some tea and cream cakes — I often wondered where all the fancy cakes came from, both there and when I was with Joy down in Maidstone. We giggled our way through the lot, but my sister was far more interested to hear how I had managed to get a lift in a truck, the only girl among a load of Yankees, all the way from Farnham to Chertsey. It had been hilarious, but I suspect the route was altered to suit my requirements that day.

I travelled up to Oxford by train where Stanley was waiting for me. The single-decker bus we caught seemed to stop anywhere on request and so I got off with him and saw "Orchard Cottage" for the first time. It was still cold and I was wearing my greatcoat, but a warm welcome awaited us. His father was an Air-Raid Warden, whilst Olive made no secret of wanting to meet me. She mentioned the subject of the gloves several times, always adding how nice it was to think that there were young girls willing to help in this way. It was soon apparent that Stanley was an "outdoor" person and in no time at all he was in a pair of wellies with his airgun in his hand, and out we went. I was later to learn that he was also quite adept at black and white pen artistry and I was to have a personal gift of "Orchard Cottage" given to me years later.

I'm ashamed to admit that coming from Surrey I had never travelled far enough away from my home to see watercress growing in beds. The garden was a place of pure enchantment to me, with a small stream meandering slowly along the bottom of it and to my utter joy, a watercress bed. I have mostly been an "indoor" type, even more so since my childhood, so Stanley's lifestyle was a whole new world to me and I was content to cease my chatter and stand quietly by to watch him. He set up a row of old cans on some garden paling and was soon taking pot shots at them. It was easy to see that he was no novice at this pastime.

He handed me the gun, the first time I had ever held one in my hands, and luckily it was to be the last.

"Go ahead, have a go," he said as he replaced the cans. I truly wished I was the sporty type, but his happy, infectious laughter and sense of fun made it sound so easy, so I lifted the gun and took aim. It turned out to be an aim to be remembered not only on this visit but for many years to come. I had shot right through his father's watering can. Of course, it was low down and the thing became totally useless as water gushed out as soon as it was filled only an inch or two. I was horrified. I guessed that buying a replacement would be impossible in wartime. My first thought was to rush back to the house and confess my accident, but Stanley just threw back his head and laughed merrily.

We turned to go back to the house and I saw a small, shy four-year-old girl watching us. I did not make the mistake of rushing at her, I knew a more gentle approach would be more effective. She did not seem to want to talk to me but after a while she came and took my hand and we all three entered the house together. Stanley still wore his impish grin but Olive wasn't fooled when she saw the look of apprehension on my face.

"Now what have you been up to?" she asked. It was to become a family joke. The watering can remained useless but Stanley's parents seemed loath to part with it.

The day was a happy one and like all happy days passed all too quickly, nevertheless I had feelings of inferiority creeping over me several times, as well as times of complete bewilderment. Olive's romanticism did not stop at me — there was much talk about a farming family with three sons and a daughter. I gathered Stanley had been to school with at least one or more of the boys, but it was the girl who interested me. She sounded a perfect match in every way for this happy, quiet, intellectual and much-loved son.

I had no right to feel possessive about Stanley, after all I had my Mac, but if we were truthful we were a little bit in love with all our friends, albeit that many were nothing more than ships that passed in the night. However, that day was to be mine, all mine, for when that night came I was to be VIP once more.

There was no suitably-timed bus back to Oxford. I discovered that Stanley was quite adept at riding his own cycle in and coming back with a second cycle running alongside. For the second time in a week, I found myself on an old-fashioned high-saddled cycle, this one belonging to Olive. We said our "Goodbyes" and left. There was plenty of time before the train left and Stanley announced quite nonchalantly that he'd call in at New College and leave the bikes with the Bursar. It was the first indication that his education had not ended at Thame Grammar School. I, who had left school at the age of fourteen, was a little excited at the prospect of even entering one of the universities — how far I had come since I had left my home town in the spring of 1941.

We walked to the railway station with time to spare, or so we thought, but after a long wait we learned that the train we were waiting for would not be running that night.

Inferior I might have felt at times but God endowed me with a fast thinking brain which sprang quickly into action when faced with a predicament. Very few people had telephones in those days, yet strangely enough my first thought was to wonder how I could contact my father. I wanted to let him know that the family of strangers (all but Stanley) that I had been visiting were very respectable and that I would have to return to their home and make another try to get home to Surrey the next morning. As we walked back to collect the two cycles I asked Stanley if he could bribe the Bursar to let me telephone my father at Farnham Police Station, and our request was granted. Having got through, I was told by the Duty Officer that my dad was out on his Special Constable's beat until ten o'clock. I asked him to assure my father that I was fine — but for the train not running I would have got back.

It was quite a while later when I learned that my dad, on receiving this message, said "My daughter has been away almost every night since she joined the WAAF, and now she rings up here to tell me she won't be home tonight." Apparently he was told by his Duty Officer that he could see my reasoning.

"You weren't expecting her home all those other nights, but you were tonight," the Duty Officer had said. "As she said, she was visiting people she didn't know, so I think she behaved in a very thoughtful way."

With that done we set off back to "Orchard Cottage", there now being no need for Stanley to cope with both cycles.

How different was this night to that snowy one when we met for the first time. We stopped off for a while and leaned on a five-barred gate, but the brilliant moon did nothing to throw us into even a mild embrace. Rather we talked of his very young sister and I remarked on her unusual name and how it was spelt — little guessing that just by doing that I was laying history in store to be used many, many years ahead.

When we arrived back at "Orchard Cottage" for the second time Stanley took the cycles round the back of the house, putting a finger over my mouth to show me that he wanted complete hush! I pressed myself hard against the side of the wall in shadow and he knocked on the front door. Everything was done in haste in those days because of the blackout regulations, yet still his impish grin gave the game away in the few seconds he stood in the light from the open door. Nothing missed Olive who was back in her romantic mood again.

"Who have you got there?" she enquired and went on to ask us if we had missed the train on purpose and how long had we been spooning in the moonlight. But to her credit she had total faith in her son's behaviour for when we went to our respective rooms in the roof she made no comment at all — if anyone was disillusioned it was I, dressed in one of Olive's nighties I was disappointed when Stanley never even popped in to kiss me good night.

My times with Stanley were to last just one short year. All my four Januarys as a WAAF were snowy and when my second snowy January rolled round in 1943, this wonderful young man who had surely snatched me from almost certain death twelve months before, was the pilot of a Lancaster with a crew of six doing Ops over Essen. On the 9th January, 1943, they were shot down and all but one it is believed, lost their lives. The survivor is thought to have been a Canadian who lived out the rest of his war years in a Prisoner of War Camp and eventually returned to his native Canada. Olive searched for him for many years but was never to find him nor even to get any details about him.

Maybe with time I could have coped but I was not then very experienced. I cannot pass lightly over the year I knew Stanley, indeed I suspect he gave me many more years to live when he threw me into that ditch full of snow the January before he died, only aged twenty-one and four months. Olive was grief-stricken and was never the same again. She never got over the loss of her son. I think this factor, like her urge to find the Canadian survivor, was in part why she always wanted me to continue to be in touch. I was someone who had shared his life and laughter and the old watering can became more precious than before. He was, perhaps, more vivacious than I have given him credit for being. He must have held me in greater regard than I had thought, for he left me many memories, among them snapshots taken in Canada where he started his training before I met him. It was to be many years before I learned three things I did not know at that time.

There was the time when he arranged for us to meet in Sheffield at "Aunty May's" — Olive and his father both hailed from that part of the country, but "Aunty May" was just a courtesy title given to a much-loved neighbour and which I was asked to use, making my short stay very informal. I arrived when everybody was out at work but was greeted by red-haired, freckle-faced Keith, who at fourteen years of age seemed to be in complete control in coping with a visitor, albeit a stranger. I was quickly served up a plate of crisply-fried eggs and chips.

Aunty May was unflappable and very quick, like Keith. Stanley arrived from his bomber station and kissed me warmly and I was just about set for spending these few unexpected hours with him, when once again I was hit by another bout of feeling inferior. I had heard that Aunty May had a son and a daughter but was quite unprepared for the pretty young woman who walked in. Her reddish hair was worn in the style of the day, long and curly, just as mine was, but dark in colour. Regulations forbade me to wear it other than wound round a piece of brown ribbon so that it was an inch above my tunic collar.

Worse was to follow. Soon I watched silently as Stanley drew out the piano stool and requested his favourite "One Fine Day" from "Madame Butterfly", though not a word had passed between them. Betty had a truly beautiful voice and I had no need to worry as the evening was to be mine, all mine. I gathered she went almost nightly to sing to the Troops from a stage somewhere in the city of Sheffield. However, Stanley always had impeccable manners, on a par with my Mac, so that after some discussion with Aunty May regarding a put-u-up for me, he asked me if I would like to go to the cinema.

Travelling by tram into the city and back was in itself a revelation to me, a mode of transport I had never seen before. We saw the film "Sun Valley Serenade" and even after all these years I can never watch a rerun of it, or listen to the Glenn Miller music and songs from it without my eyes brimming with tears. But there were no tears that night.

I was fated to see Stanley once again in an even more surprising fashion. I was still in the Orderly Room one evening when I was told that there was a telephone call for me, a rare event indeed for someone of my humble rank. It was ages before they made me believe that it was not a leg-pull and that Stanley had landed at Tern Hill and was way out at Dispersal. I very quickly twigged that it was a case of the least said the better, so we arranged time and place of meeting and when we did meet I think it must have been the absurdity of it all that threw us into each other's arms. An Officer had decided to make a false landing, had run out of fuel and had asked if anyone was interested in making the trip. Hence, I had my last, though of course I did not know it, loving "Goodbye" to a young man who was soon to die.

Olive would not be convinced that her son would do such a thing and always accused me of telling her a fairy-tale. Years later, long after the war had ended, when she finally let me see, not just his discs, but the sixty-nine letters of condolence and his Log Book, I learned those three facts that I had never known before. Even I was surprised as I pointed out to Olive the entry in his Log Book about his false landing at Tern Hill, even I had not expected it to be recorded.

Then Olive said two surprising things to me. "I always keep your letter on the top of the pile," she told me. "I wondered how someone could write such an expressive letter at such a tender age. I think he did love you, Eileen, because when his sister couldn't say Stanley she used her own childish version which he never allowed anyone outside the family to use, yet you referred to him by it in your last letter to me."

I did not tell her that I had written to him and called him thus, nine days after he was killed. The letter was never returned. Olive was delighted when I named my only daughter, many years later, after that small four-year-old sister I had first set eyes on on that fateful, happy day when I had shot through their watering can on my first visit to "Orchard Cottage" in 1942. My daughter knows that but for Stanley she might well not have been born my offspring, but equally she knows about my Mac too.

CHAPTER NINE

CORPORAL STAPLEY

My year with Stanley was but twelve months made up of scattered instances, but my life went on at Tern Hill after he left at the end of February, when his Flying Training there was over. I did go to the party for number 67 Course and remember we all got a bit sloshed, but not nearly, in my case, as much as when I went down to Wolverhampton by truck to some big dance.

My most vivid memory of that night was how I was impressed by the width of the stairs and that huge plants in pots were on each side of about every third stair. I was on gin and lime, as usual, but was far from being drunk because I remember the laughter when I suddenly felt sick.

"Please excuse me," I said and to everyone's utter amazement I went calmly over to one of the pots and vomited, then returned and said, in all innocence "Ah, that feels a lot better!" But I did not really enjoy drink and still only smoked a maximum of five cigarettes a day just to feel I was in the swing of things. Mind you, when your hands are occupied with a typewriter it does mercifully restrict one. Later I decided to attend only the Christmas parties, held in the Sergeants' Mess, or the dances occasionally held in Market Drayton.

Joy and I were venturing on long hitchhikes about this time, completely ignoring the thirty mile radius, of course. I well remember us reaching Rhyl in N. Wales, but our most outstanding trip was when we were picked up by a lorry driver, when we had made no plans as to where we were heading for, and it was he who suggested we join him and go to Southport. Youth is crazy, we had no idea of mileage, it just seemed like a good idea — but I was always the one who worried as to how we would get back, or even if we would! It turned out to be a really fantastic trip, made all the more memorable when the driver told us we were coming up to Ormskirk.

"I'm going to break the regulations for you here," he said, much to our astonishment. "We're not supposed to go up this way, but I want to show you something really unusual." He pulled up by a church and asked us if we could see what was unusual about it, but though we looked very hard at it we could not spot its oddity. "I'd better point it out to you, as I don't want to be caught here where I'm not supposed to be," said the driver and pointed out that the mainly perpendicular church carries two west towers, one of which bears a spire and contains interesting effigies in the Derby Chapel, which of course we could not stop to see. The driver moved off and as he drove on he told us that he had been told that the reason for the two towers was that two sisters had left money towards the building of the church, but they had a difference of opinion. One wanted a spire and the other a tower, hence the reason for it having both — but the driver told us that he was not sure if that was the truth of the matter. I was very impressed by the fact that a man who earned his living as a lorry driver should not only be so knowledgeable but that he had gone out of his way to share his knowledge with two young WAAFs.

There were other places we hitched to, but sadly I gave up when I had a very frightening experience on that same road I had hitched to Shrewsbury and had shared a happy day there with an Army Officer's wife. I was not so lucky next time I went alone. I sat up in the tall lorry and never really felt at ease from the start. Real fear struck me when this driver turned off the main road and we were going down a rutted sort of farm road.

"Oh, no. No, please!" I said in horror as I looked out at the barren fields and countryside, the hedges stripped of their greenery and not a soul in sight.

I went to open the door of the lorry on my side. It was very high and would have been an immense drop.

"No, don't do that," said the driver. "I did this to teach you a lesson. I have a daughter about your age and I thought what could happen to young people like you and the danger you run." He started backing out.

"I will take you to Shrewsbury just this once, but only if you promise not to hitchhike with someone who might do you harm," he ordered.

"Thank you," I said, "I am really shaking with fright," but he just patted my hand and we went on in silence.

On the rare occasions I found that there were young men I had danced with at a small social club in Farnham, I always went, whenever I could by public transport. I met one in Leek, Staffs., who wrote to me later from Australia, and another one I had always had a soft spot for prewar, in Wolverhampton. We had been Leading Aircraftwomen quite some time as the test did not involve typing, just paperwork which we all seemed to find easy to cope with.

There was one memorable day when Joy and I found ourselves hitching lifts somewhere in Worcestershire and we were surprised to be picked up by a very "out of the top drawer" sort of driver. His car was big and blue but not being mechanically bent I could not even hazard a guess as to what make it was, only that it was huge and very, very comfortable. It was rare also because Joy was the one this jolly, rotund driver had selected to sit beside him on the front seat. It was another gorgeously sunny day, so I was content just to relax in such a swish car. I was so happy that I found I was not even interested in the chatter going on up front, until suddenly the gentleman's words both reached and surprised me.

"Do you know," he was saying to Joy, "I'm looking for a lovely, small young WAAF for my son. It's about time he married and you look to be a very likely candidate." I was just about to start feeling alarmed when he drove his beautiful car between some others to the left of the entrance of a lovely ivy-covered, fairly large hotel.

"Come on, out you get," he said and led us inside. I did not catch the words passed between him and the Head Waiter, but like magic a table for the three of us was soon found and we were enjoying some really good English cooking and he chose some wine to go with it. What I enjoyed most was the homely atmosphere and the fact that the pudding was syrup treacle sponge with custard sauce. Before we left he led us over to the window and we looked down on the adjoining old Benedictine Priory, a really beautiful sight, we then set off in the direction of Tern Hill. Joy might well have forgotten this jolly matchmaking rotund gentleman and maybe I would have done so too had it not been for the fact that I was being driven round a bend in the road years later and I suddenly cried out "Oh, look, that is the ivy-covered hotel where Joy and I lunched with a perfect stranger about forty years ago."

I was taken in for lunch there for a second time and there were to be two coincidences. The pudding was syrup treacle sponge, among other varieties, and I was treated to a small round brass frame holding dried flowers, as a souvenir. As I turned it over to date it I found it to be 3rd September 1980, the forty-first anniversary of the outbreak of the Second World War. But I ran into trouble when I staked my claim to have lunched there with another WAAF as guests of a gentleman, a complete stranger.

"Oh, no madam, you must be mistaken," I was told. I was adamant and I said it would have been the summer of 1942, and that it bore the same name "The Abbey Hotel" Worcestershire.

After a while he said "Ah, yes, I see you could be right, you were wearing uniform I take it? Well, there was a period around that time when "The Boffins" used this place for a short while and so had entitlement to use the restaurant and to account for any visitors they invited to meals." I suddenly found myself an object of interest for a few minutes, for this "Boffin" remained silent about the affair. Joy was never to learn the truth of that day and for me it was surely 'serendipity' I suppose, a truly happy chance find.

Outside I took a long look and pictured that other sunny day and the blue car just where it had been all those years ago. Joy would have been delighted had she known we were treated to a free luncheon by a "Boffin" — yes, I'm sure she would have loved to have known that!

Reaching the rank of Leading Aircraftwoman was not all that difficult as we were all considered to be sufficiently proficient at typing and so had only paperwork to cope with. As I said, the greatest advantage was that it gave a WAAF her first visible sign of her ranking. We wore propellers on our sleeves, but though I likened it to being a Lance Corporal in the Army, I never felt it had quite the clout.

However, the rank of LACW did bring with it a duty, no matter what one's trade. I have great cause to remember this fact. One night Joy and I paired off, as was normal, to share being Night Duty Clerks in HQ. I was miffed that, as we were both LACWs, Joy was claiming seniority, which meant I would be the one to go to the NAAFI to collect our Night Duty Suppers. But it did not turn out quite the way Joy had anticipated — yes! I was to become VIP once again.

I watched as she picked up the telephone then saw her blanch as she said "Yes, Sir" two or three times. Before I had time to ask her she blurted out "Oh, my God, that was the CO — he wants a message put out over the Tannoy."

"So?" I asked, "what's your problem, we have all been trained to meet this emergency."

"It's no use" she said "I simply can't do it. You'll have to come with me into the Adjutant's Office."

"You know the rules" I said, "one of us must remain in the Orderly Room to answer the telephone."

Try as I might, I could not get her to budge and, conscious that time was ticking by, I caved in and told her to get her skates on. We went into the Adjutant's Office together. Looking back, I can see just how simple it should have been, but some of her panic had rubbed off on me.

There was a board on the wall bearing four switches, two red and two green. I sat next to her in one of the two chairs facing the switches and watched as she leaned forward to put down the two red ones which would set off the humming warning all over the camp that a message was imminent — that a broadcast was about to be made. So far, so good, but then I watched in horror as she leaned forward and, instead of switching the green ones on, she switched the red ones OFF.

"What the devil do you think you're playing at?" I asked.

"It's no use, I simply can't do it at all, you'll have to do it" she said.

So I was to become VIP once more. I could feel mild panic welling up in me as I became more and more conscious of time passing. We exchanged chairs and I leaned forward to switch the red switches down again. It's now or never, I was thinking, but as I leaned forward to switch down the green switches I took a deep breath and out popped a short nervous giggle. After that all went well. I went into the normal routine of saying "Calling all Ranks, calling all Ranks, here is a message from the Commanding Officer." I then proceeded to give out the message in a slow clear voice, ending with "End of Message — over and out."

I do not have the least idea as to what I said "On Air" that night; I just remember that when I went to the NAAFI to collect our Night Duty Suppers, a member of HQ Staff approached me. "Was that you on the Tannoy just now, Eileen, what happened when the red ones were switched off?"

Ignoring that, I asked "Was I OK?" and he replied "Yes, after the short nervous giggle it was loud and clear and a credit to you."

I had expected that it would be Joy who would be called for by the Adjutant next morning — but, oh dear me no, it was to be me.

"Hello" was his greeting, "what happened to Adgy last night?"

I said "Sorry, Sir, but she went into panic, so I thought quickly and decided that I had better take over."

"Well, I must say, you do your best to have a go at everything; after your little nervous giggle the message was loud and clear and you remembered not to gabble."

"Thank you, Sir," I said. Then as I stood with my hand on the handle of his office door I turned back and said "I must surely be the WAAF who has been to visit you more times than any other."

He smiled and said "Yes, and never twice on the same subject."
So I was to remember the duty that came with the Rank of LACW
— (Leading/Aircraftwoman)!

I cannot give an exact date to the evening when our Sergeant was
looking out of one of the tall windows.

"Eileen," he said, "your boyfriend is waiting," then added
quickly "no, I've made a mistake."

"Well, is it, or isn't it?" I asked. "You ought to know by now."
I went across to join him and saw to my horror the reason for his
thinking he was wrong — it was my Mac but in his cap he wore the
white flash denoting Aircrew. I grabbed my jacket — my feet
hardly touched the stairs as I ran down them, pulling on my jacket
as I rushed in great haste to reach him, but long before that my eyes
were already brimming with tears. I had always suspected that Mac
had a yen to join Aircrew in some capacity, mainly a pilot, I
thought.

"Oh, no! Oh, no!" I said as he took my hand as usual and
brushed my tear-stained cheek. He said nothing but just hugged me
close to him. I think maybe it was a tussle for him too — he could
do one but only at the expense of not doing the other. I had always
said that I did not want him to fly, I wanted him to remain ground
crew and stay with me. I had always cushioned myself with the fact
that it was more difficult for a "Boy Entrant" to succeed as they
were considered as being fully trained in their Ground Duties. But
in a few weeks the flash was missing.

I knew that he did not want to hurt me and that he would hide his
true feelings by teasing me, so I was not surprised when he said
"You know I was unable to be with you last night, I was on duty in
the Officers' Mess where there was a big 'do' and as I was serving
the CO with his soup my flash fell out of my cap into his soup!"

"Oh, Mac, such nonsense," I replied. "You would not be
wearing a cap indoors anyway." He remained mute on the subject
whilst I rejoiced in the knowledge that he would not be leaving me
yet.

I passed the O/R Sergeant as I went into work next morning.
"Did he tell you?" he asked me.

"No," I said, "I got what I expected, his usual teasing with a
load of old rubbish."

Sergeant looked hard at me. "All this has been a great blow to
you, hasn't it, Eileen?" Just the usuage of my name during
working hours showed that he cared. "You won't get any peace
until you know, will you? I'll see what I can find out in the
Sergeants' Mess at lunch time."

I was impatient for his return and he had learned the truth, but now is not the time to relate it. Sufficient to say it was not for any misdemeanor on the part of Mac, so I pretended I did not know the reason, and I knew one must never betray a trust, anyway.

So I had Mac back as Ground Staff for a few more blissfully, happy weeks, but then I lost Joy. She had left Tern Hill as she had requested a posting to one of our Satellite Dromes. I knew it could not last because these were really passionate years, full of movement and a mixture everchanging of meetings and partings, happiness and sadness, sometimes death bringing a terrible sense of loss, but moments of personal happiness until another day would dawn and snatch it all away.

Once again we looked down at Mac waiting for me, once more sporting a white Aircrew flash. I knew it would be for real this time and the thought of his going to another training school left me shattered. But what happened next seemed to be a mixture of the lot. Mac was such a poor correspondent, so I knew I could at best only hope for an occasional postcard, or maybe nothing at all. Little did I guess that I was in for an even greater surprise. I passed Sergeant sitting at his usual place up on the dais on the end nearest the door.

"Good morning, Corporal," he said. Thinking he had made a slip I just kept walking and took no notice. "I said good morning Corporal," he said again.

"Yes, I heard you, but you're a bit premature aren't you?" I replied.

"No, as from the promulgation of today's PORs you will be Corporal Stapley, the youngest WAAF Corporal on the station."

I was staggered. "I just can't believe it," I said. "When did all this happen?"

"The Adjutant and I discussed it several weeks ago and we both reached the conclusion that you have covered all you will learn here in the Orderly Room, so all that remains is for me to offer you my congratulations then break the sad news to you that you cannot stay here in HQ, otherwise we will have too many Captains and not enough Crew."

I was to wonder often whether this gentle, kind-hearted man who had initiated my move from the Station Cookhouse, had been my mentor to make me proficient enough at my trade to become a Corporal at such a young age, had seen fit to suggest my promotion when Mac had received his white flash the first time, so that I would be even more busy when the time for his eventual leaving came. I was to pack straight away. I was told, as I had been allocated to the Engineering Section.

"Oh, my God," I blasphemed, "I don't have the remotest knowledge of engineering," but all I got was a wry smile and a reminder that I was Clerk/GENERAL DUTIES!

I gathered together my few personal items and said a quiet goodbye to each member of staff. Having arrived to work in HQ from the kitchen in such a surprising fashion I now found myself equally surprised in the manner of my leaving it. I certainly was not instantly aware of the great honour that had been bestowed on me. I had been used to working as an underling in P.3 and it was sometime before I realized that I was now responsible to two Engineering Officers, one a Squadron Leader, the other a Flight Lieutenant, and that I also had a staff of three. Nothing like throwing one in at that deep end, I thought!

Only the Squadron Leader was in the office when I reported for duty and he floored me straight away.

"Who are you?" he asked.

"Corporal Stapley, Sir," I replied and he immediately contradicted me.

"Oh, no you're not, a Corporal wears chevrons on her sleeves. I have been promised a WAAF Corporal and that is what I want."

"I didn't know myself until I arrived in the Orderly Room this morning, Sir, and in any case I am not officially a Corporal until today's PORs are promulgated."

I think he decided to call that quits. "How old are you, Stapley?" he asked.

"Nineteen, Sir, but I will be twenty in August."

"That's very young, isn't it? You must remember to act with decorum at all times. Now I think you had better slip along to Stores and collect your stripes, then go to your Billet and bring back that thing you WAAFs call a 'Housewife' and get stitching straight away." Everyone hated being seen as a "Rookie" Corporal and most would rub their glaring white chevrons in dirt to make them look well worn.

My Staff was comprised of Bill, who, having been in the Sally Army in Civvy Street, was often absent attending Band Practice. My Clerk/Typist was another Eileen and came from Birmingham. She still pronounced the hard 'g' on such words as singing and talking. She was Irish or of Irish descent, hence her name of Eileen, unlike mine, was bestowed on her for this reason. A touch of old Ireland with a "brummy" accent!

Lastly there was Ricky; I never knew him by any other name. He was my "Runner", in other words he ran messages and did other odd jobs, when he could be found! Rank didn't hold much sway with Ricky, but his accent totally fascinated me as he came from Bradford, which he always referred to as 'Bratford'.

Yet it was Ricky who was to make my first morning as an NCO really memorable.

It soon became apparent that he seemed to know only two sentences. Each morning at eleven-thirty he would pipe up with "I'm now off — early lunch" — and likewise at four-thirty he merely changed it to "I'm now off — early tea." But it was Ricky who was ready for me that first morning; when he returned he spoke to me and was the first person to address me as Corporal. "You won't enjoy your lunch today, Corporal," he said and, of course, I fell right in it!

"Why ever not?" I asked.

"Oh, it's the workmen in the Mess," he said.

"Are you telling me that men are working in the Mess at the same time that we are expected to eat?"

"It's the sawdust you won't like" he said. "It gets all over the food."

I couldn't believe this conversation. "You mean they are making sawdust in the Mess whilst we are eating?" I persisted. "Whatever can be so important that it can't wait until after lunch? What are they doing?"

"They're widening the doors to get your head through," he said with a wicked grin. There was nothing else to do but laugh, but I had a long memory as he was to find out sometime in the future.

I cannot pretend that I got off to a good start workwise either. On that first morning it was the wrath of the F/Lt I brought around my ears. Not having had time to learn to touch type I was simply not acquainted with shorthand at all. He wrote his first letter in longhand for me to type and, feeling that I had to make up for my inadequacy, I set to work determined to show him that I was worth my salt. When I had completed my task I took the utmost care when reading it through — it was well spaced on the paper, the Reference and Date were correct — so all was well I thought. I left for my late lunch and smiled when I noticed that there was no sign of a workman anywhere! How different when I returned — it was as if we had a raging bull next door. The hatch was thrown open and I was greeted with "What the hell do you think this means?" I went out of our door, passed our office window, beside which sat the other Eileen and went in to enquire what was wrong. I, who had never heard any Engineering Technology had misread the Flight/Lieutenant's handwriting and instead of "Reference your hand turning gear" had typed "Reference your hard tinning gear". But as the days passed we all quickly found ourselves talking about Airframes and Engine changes, Ailerons and a hundred and one other engineering terms. Even crashes became "prangs". I helped out with the typing quite a lot and got into the habit of sitting opposite to Eileen so that I was facing the hatch. I also got into the habit of sitting with my left leg tucked up under me as I typed. How I wish I had listened to Bill's frequent warnings that one day I would regret this habit and end up suffering from a bad back.

There was little more to say about Ricky, he just came and went, doing as little as possible but in such a lovable, friendly way that I found myself overlooking his frequent and often long periods of absence. Eileen was a different kettle of fish. Two facts concerning her are lodged in my mind. The first was her way of saving her breath by greeting us with "Good morning, each apiece."

The second was funny to behold. One morning she altered her routine and I thought she had 'flipped her lid' when she threw open the office door, flung out her right arm wide and said in a loud clear voice, as if an actress "The deed is done — where shall I put the dagger?" We were all on the point of laughing when the hatch was opened and one of the Officers called out "Never mind the bloody dagger — get on with some work!" It was quite soon that my desk was moved into the Officers' Office thus making me more available for taking telephone calls in case of emergency. I got to know both of them very well and discovered our "grumpy" Flight Lieutenant was very nice when one got to know him.

The poor Squadron Leader was a martyr to sinus trouble and I was forever dashing off to get what medical aid I could muster. When he was fit he had a wicked sense of humour. Arriving back from lunch one day he enquired what I was doing and when I told him I was "turning out my drawers" his reply was unprintable.

When Mac left there were no tears, because I did not see him leave. He could not bring himself to face our parting because inwardly he was torn apart with his need to fly and his love for me. Of course there were times when gnawing doubts assailed me, but he had never even glanced at another WAAF and I had his beautiful studio portrait beside my bed signed "Lots of Love — Mac". He had been just twenty-three years old that May when we met in 1941 and I still had three months to go to my nineteenth birthday. But I was shattered and having the keys to the office I made work my salvation, evenings included. My new rank brought me extra responsibility.

At last, when I went home on leave, my father, who for many

years had served as a regular soldier across in France and Belgium, winning for himself some very distinguished medals, could get to grips with my rank. After all the Army had Corporals. He was so proud that, never having had a son, he did at last have a daughter with chevrons on her sleeves and I suppose he was to be forgiven his pride when he talked of me as if I were some famous General!

Our office looked out on the airfield and far away in the distance was the Wrekin. I shuddered whenever there was a "prang". The thought that some young life was lost before being fully trained was very daunting and even worse if it was the life of someone one knew, so I think I subconsciously made up my mind that I would never again lose my heart to anyone connected with flying. I remained hard working and lonely.

CHAPTER TEN

"Q"

It came about that a Corporal Radio or Wireless Operator asked me for a date and I accepted. We had seen each other many times, as his office and workshop, like our office, ran alongside one of the hangars. We were supposed to adhere to the rule of using paths but most of us took our lives in our hands and wove ourselves between the aircraft in for repair. Again I found myself with an only son, but he was also an only child too. He was an ex-Grammar School lad from the north and it was obvious from the start that he was far more attracted to me than I to him.

One of our earliest dates was when we met to go to Market Drayton, where we intended to change buses, go first to the Potteries and then on to Trentham Gardens. He is still living and so I shall just refer to him as "Q".

We set off, sitting on the back seat. I had never mentioned my affair with Mac, so it was a feeling of *déjà vu* when he reached out and held my hand. It was to prove to be "Q" 's initiation into my being VIP, because after a while I asked him if he could smell something burning, but he couldn't so I knelt up on the back seat to look out of rear window to see huge flames coming out of the back of the bus. We shouted to the driver and eventually we were all requested to vacate the bus.

"That was some passion between you two on the back seat," the driver quipped.

"But we were only holding hands," I replied, embarrassed.

I need only tell you a little of that gloriously sunny day, and that it is the day I will always associate with "Q". I can still visualise us as we were when we walked into Trentham Gardens. He was holding my hand as we looked at the sun-sparkled water in the swimming pool. The song coming through the Tannoy was "Roses of Picardy". Strange, how just one song can take you back across the years and remind you of a special day. So this was to be forever in my mind, his place and his song. At that time I thought that it was a pity that Mac had not left me with a special piece of music. With Stanley it had been Glenn Miller, with "Q" it would always be "Roses of Picardy" which already had an extra special meaning for me because of my father's long spell across the water during the First World War.

Our dates continued and I did nothing to stop them yet was always aware that perhaps I ought to speak.

There came a night when I was on some NCO duty then just as I was expecting to see "Q" the following night I was asked by the Squadron Leader when I arrived at the office if I had a date. I replied in the affirmative.

"Well, you haven't any more," he responded. "You will be baby-sitting for the W/Co tonight. There is a big "do" on tonight in the Officers' Mess."

Of course, I argued and even dared to call him a "Creep" because the Wing Commander was allocated a male Sergeant, but I knew I would have to go. Later in the day I returned to WAAF quarters and collected my night attire, toothbrush etc. It was to have its funny side for all that, for as I sat in the back of the Wing Commander's big car and it swept out through the main gates I watched with interest as the men on guard duty gave some spiffing salutes. As I turned round to glance out of the rear window I was recognised and could hardly keep my composure as I watched each of them give the wrong type of Victory "V" — now well known as being a "Harvey Smith".

We arrived at the house, a large one set in beautiful woods, but I was made aware of my rank immediately when I was shown to the kitchen. It was a very cosy room and I was served with a lovely meal of roast chicken with all the trimmings. My bedroom for the night was a chintz affair with curtains to match the very pretty bedspread. It almost made the experience worthwhile — a long way forward from my humble beginning in the Station Cookhouse to being a WAAF Corporal spending a night baby-sitting in a Wing Commander's big house. Next I was taken to meet the family, three boys, already each in a bed but all in the same room. The Wing Commander and his wife left, leaving me to discover that their youngest son, aged about seven, suffered with St Vitus's dance. I seemed to spend my whole evening going up and down the stairs in an effort to settle him and that became the night when a seven-year-old boy taught me that my usage of the English language left much to be desired.

E

Slightly annoyed with him I spoke sharply saying "Lay down."

He answered quickly "It's not lay down, you ought to know by now it is 'lie down'."

Having voted me for this mission, Squadron Leader was not in good humour when we all had a nice lie-in the following morning, followed by a leisurely breakfast, and so we were late returning to camp. I was ready for my return trip back through the main gates and this time I turned round and stuck out my tongue — a wee moment to forget decorum at all times.

I met "Q" between two hangars later that day and after listening to my previous night's happenings he told me that he and one of his staff, whom I did know slightly, had been out cycling and it was then that I realised just how caring he was about me.

"You would love it there, it would remind you of Surrey, all gorse and heather. Would you like me to take you there tonight?"

"Surely you'd rather go elsewhere?" I said. But it was obvious that he had his mind set already on making me this offer, so I accepted and arranged time and place to meet with our cycles. I have never had a great sense of direction, still haven't for that matter, so I have no idea which way we took as we left camp. I always bubbled away and left navigational matters to others. The first thing I recall was reaching a sandy gully so evocative of Surrey that I at last became aware of our surroundings. We had to dismount to push the cycles.

"Look, look up on the bank," he said suddenly and for the first time since leaving my home I was conscious of the beauty of Surrey and even felt a little homesick.

"Q" threw both the cycles up on the bank and we climbed up and sat amongst the heather. I threw off my cap and dropped my long, curly hair from its brown ribbon and wallowed in the familiar perfumes of my childhood.

"It's lovely," I said, "really lovely and very unselfish of you to come two nights running."

"Eileen, you must know by now that I think you are lovely too, you must surely know how I feel about you." He leaned over gently to kiss me as he had done a few times before; but this time it was with an intensity he had never shown before. His sudden passion took me by surprise but even more surprisingly he suddenly said "Oh, no, I mustn't touch you" and quickly got up and walked away. For a while I did not move, my uniform remained untouched and I sensed that he had not brought me here for any purpose other than the reason he had given. I sat up and twisted my hair round its ribbon and after a while he came quietly back to me and sat down beside me.

"Forgive me, please? I'm really sorry, it's just that I care for you so very much."

"Yes, I know you do and you proved how caring you are by getting up and walking away," I said.

We only stayed long enough to vow to each other that such a situation would never occur again — and it never did.

Life continued much as before and it was Christmas once more. I found myself with plenty of dancing partners in the Sergeants' Mess and it seemed livelier than the previous year, but maybe this was because I was another year older. I did not hear from Mac and supposed he had gone to Scotland to join his mother for his Christmas/Hogmanay leave. It was now almost a year since that snowy night of January, 1942, when Stanley had saved my life. But life can be very cruel at times, so I supposed I was blessed that I was not to know that just nine days into this coming New Year of 1943, his life would come to its end and that Olive would remain totally devastated and never get over the loss of her dearly-loved son.

Life went on at Tern Hill too and I was staggered when both of my Engineering Officers were posted. It was just a short while before their departures that I learned down the grapevine that my stunning-looking actor, John Justin, was leaving soon, too. There had been a rule enforced that in future no WAAFs were to go up flying, not even if they were mechanics, but news reached me that the prettiest one, a stunning brunette with one of those fancy names I always so envied, did go up and when the plane landed she was green with airsickness and F/O Ledesma had lifted her in his arms and carried her across the airfield.

"Just my luck to be stuck in this office with no hope of seeing him let alone getting his autograph," I said to my Squadron Leader. I had to explain that I had known since my early days back in the Orderly Room that he was really John Justin, the actor.

To my total surprise he promptly lifted the telephone and asked that F/O Ledesma report to him before he left camp, but was told that he was up flying again and the Squadron Leader's message would be passed on when he landed. Hours seemed to pass by and my ever-ready autograph book lay open in readiness for the great moment that was soon to be mine. Lunch time came and the two Officers went to their Mess but I sat on. I feared I would miss my lunch if he did not turn up soon, but I was finally defeated by a call of nature so strong that I was powerless to wait any longer. I decided that by now he would have gone to the Officers' Mess for his lunch too, but I was wrong. I was fated never to meet my idol for when I returned there was my autograph book where I had left it and written in it was: 'To Eileen Stapley, with very best wishes from John Justin', and underneath, bless him, he had written 'Not (F/O Ledesma, to you.)' So he had been told of my long wait and that I had known from the day he signed in who he really was. I have always been faithful to him for that memorable occasion and over the years watch any reruns of his early-day films, but I never saw him when he was so very young and handsome, just that fleeting glance as he looked back at the trestle table where I was sitting with Corporal Tom all that long time ago.

It seemed to be a time for movement and just as I had found that promotion has a debit side too, so "Q" learned that his promotion to Sergeant was prior to his being posted to India. We had often joked about our birthdays being four days apart and he had once suggested that if ever we had a child it would be nice if it was born on 22nd August, but I did not realise that this was meant to convey his intention of marriage. It was now some months since we had begun spending almost all our spare evenings together and I was aware that he had a great affection for me. He was not in the least like Mac, he had a stronger personality altogether and he showed his feelings. Since that night in the heather he had always treated me with the same respect as both Mac and Stanley had. I thought that I had been incredibly lucky to find three perfect gentlemen. He was in fact on the point of asking me to spend a leave by going with him to meet his parents, when his promotion and posting came quite out of the blue. It was the type of life we lived and nothing was forever it seemed. So very soon he was gone and I was on my own again.

I certainly knew most of the countryside around and the railway stations too. It had been quite early on in my service that I recall my leaving Snow Hill, in Birmingham, and the almost panic I felt when I was struggling with my kit down the cobblestones and young boys accosted me saying "Carry your bags for a penny, lady?" — but of one thing I became quite certain "That if all roads lead to Rome" then surely all trains stopped at Crewe.

I was once volunteered to play netball at nearby RAF Shawbury. They just had to be desperate — for sport was not my scene at all. There was, however, one outstanding evening when a truckload was got together and we went to the dance hall in the village of Hodnet. It was made memorable for me only because it had been pretty dull until the pubs turned out. I was sitting with a few other WAAFs when a soldier, slightly the worse for drink, made a beeline for me and even worse there was no way we could hush his noise until I acquiesced and allowed him to sit on my lap. He was getting quite weighty so I was pleased when he decided he wanted to dance with me. He was a truly handsome young man and he did seem to be coping until he suddenly stopped right in the middle of the dance floor and to my surprise he drew out a beautiful postcard-sized colour photograph of himself and started insisting I have it. We were still passing it to and fro when there was a call from the doorway announcing that our truck was about to leave. I was to keep that photograph for many years though I never did learn the young soldier's name and it went in my book as "Cavalier Unknown". With time I decided to get rid of it but I often wished I had not for men as handsome as he was do not come two a penny.

When my Officers left, they each wrote in my autograph book and to my amazement, recalling the hash I had made of Flight Lieutenant's letter that first morning, I was surprised to see he had written "Best of Luck, Luscious". The Squadron Leader chose an apposite comment on the many times I had nursed him through his many miserable hours of sinus trouble: "Oh, woman in our hours of ease, Coy, uncertain, hard to please, But when pain and anguish wring the brow, Administering Angel, thou!" So it seemed that in his own peculiar way the Flight Lieutenant had grown fond of me too — and that my "Hard tinning" gear was at last laid to rest.

We had only one Officer as replacement, another Squadron Leader. He was very much "Out of the top drawer" to my way of thinking. An early riser, he was often up by 5 a.m. and away on his own horse, which he had managed to get stabled locally somewhere. By the time we arrived for our 8.30 start he had often just returned from a thirty-mile gallop round the Wrekin. He was a quiet man, tall and rather pale for all of his outdoor activity, but though I found him difficult to understand I liked him nonetheless. He appeared to be serious all the time yet left one suspecting he might well have used a leg-pull — one beyond one's ken.

It was early in June, 1943 when Eileen came back from a visit to the Wing Commander's Office which was alongside the next hangar.

"I've just heard some news about you," she whispered very quietly. "I could not help it, nobody noticed I was in the office and so I just heard what was said. Remember the Wing Commander's Sergeant went on an NCO's Course some while back?" I nodded, so she continued, "Well it seems you are to be sent on the same type of course for WAAFs." She didn't stop, so I let her proceed for she seemed a bit agitated. "I'm furious," she said. "Do you know what cheeky remark he made about you? — he said he didn't know why they were sending such a giddy girl like you, that you only like to have fun and enjoy life and that you would only let the station down."

"Thank you," I said. "You did right to tell me, forewarned is forearmed and I'll prove him to be wrong." I knew his pass mark had been in the lower sixties, which rated a "B" pass but whether I meant it or whether it was sheer bravado I don't know.

CHAPTER ELEVEN

REDCAR

Her facts were correct and I left a few days later to attend a clerical course which ran from 20th June until early July and was held at Redcar, Yorkshire. Could this have been the journey which I recall as taking me through the long tunnel under the Pennines, leaving me lonely and a little afraid — well I've confessed that my geography was at that time very faulty, so I may be right or wrong about that. I recall how bleak and barren were the steep rises as the train sped on its way and I was filled with a great sympathy for the sheep trying to graze. How very different it all was to my green and lush Surrey. I recall passing through Whitby and thinking how chilly and windy it was for June and I wondered what my sister who was nursing in Chertsey would think if she knew I was so far from home and more especially if she was enjoying her birthday.

At last I hove up at Redcar and found we were billeted in a large, old house not far from the seafront which I supposed had been commandeered for this purpose.

We were a mixed bunch. I had expected us all to be of the rank of Corporal but almost half were still wearing their Leading Aircraftwomen Props.

I was allocated to room 5, a number I had always thought to be my destiny number, so I was pleased to find there were five occupants and that three of us, Elizabeth, Ethel and I all had names beginning with the fifth letter of the alphabet. The other two were Ruth, who was another Corporal and a Scottie, and Irene Benson. Luckily my new determination held firm right from the very first day. Since we did not know each other — though time was to alter this — we sat next to anyone in class and tended to stay with that person throughout the whole course. There was a silly expression much used about that time which I never understood because it was "Stap Me" and it was often directed at me because of my surname.

To the utter amazement of both of us the WAAF who shared the same desk was named Rosemary Stapleton and so she also had the same problem, indeed, in no time at all we were christened "The Staps" and I think we grew to quite like it.

I liked Rosemary from the start. She also was a Corporal and it was obvious that she intended to get her head down and get on with it. However, I was in for a surprise one morning when we went down to the seafront to do our daily marching stint, as much for exercise as to remind us of our initial training at Gloucester. Without being vain, I was really good at marching and what is more I thoroughly enjoyed it, so I was often found leading the group. On this particular morning I heard a voice behind me on the parade say "Well, Stap me," so naturally I wasn't very surprised, that was until we were given the "about turn" order and I happened to glance at the number on the gas mask worn by the WAAF in front of me. I could hardly believe my eyes for it was the number 442963, the number given to the girl I had pushed ahead of me in Kingsway House in order that I could become 442964.

"Stap me, too!" I whispered back. I had never known her name, but later I discovered she joined our list of names starting with the letter "E" as it was Eleanor Bird — I think those closest to her more probably called her "Birdy". I have a snapshot of her standing with another WAAF on the front steps of the house. Her first words were "My God, you've been rushing it, haven't you? How on earth have you managed to remuster to Clerk/GD and come on this course as a Corporal? How long have you had your tapes?" She really was impressed, especially when she learned that I had held my rank for so long and would not be twenty-one until 24th August, impressed but full of praise for me!

I got many autographs. Betty Durrant wrote "May you have happy memories of a holiday by the sea! Course 17, Redcar," but my favourite quote came from Elizabeth, the one in Room 5, for it was about the time of the now renowned film "Casablanca" released the year before, in 1942, with its haunting melody "As Time Goes By" and from it Elizabeth just quoted after a couple of musical notes, " 'It's still the same old story' Elizabeth, Room 5, Redcar," and this seemed to sum up the period that we spent there to perfection.

There was another incident which took place on the seafront one morning. All the elderly would sit on seats to await our arrival, almost as if it was their little treat for the day. I was in my usual position in the front and on the order to "Quick March" I set off in my best military style. It was even more windy than usual so I did not hear the "about turn" and just kept striding out. From the corner of my eye I suddenly saw several elderly men and women making pointing signals with their fingers in a frantic effort to try to get me to realise that I was marching all alone. Suddenly I heard the Drill Corporal's shout: "Where are you going — on leave?"

Was my face red as I hastened to join the Squad, but my main concern was to wonder how many marks I might have lost that morning.

Missing our mail when we were away was a hardship we had to endure. "Q" was a prolific writer and never ceased to remind me in each of his letters how much he loved me. Of course there were his views on India and as much as he dared tell me about his life out there, but he always ended by telling me how unhappy he was out there and how much he longed to be back with me.

I had not reached this far through the war without some personal tragedy. There had been the time, early on, when I was in P.3 and Corporal Tom had caught me crying over news I had received from home. He reported this fact to the Sergeant. My dad was very seriously ill with Mastoiditis which was spreading rapidly. I was a real "rookie" then and did not realise that such news was sufficiently serious for me to be granted compassionate leave, but it was, and soon I was on my way home with a leave pass to cover me for several days off. His nurse remarked that just seeing me there in my uniform had cheered him up quite a lot, though much later in the war he eventually had to give up his post as Special Constable through ill health, but this was not until 1944.

Another time I was on my way to Farnham Station after some leave when I met my cousin Reg. He was nearly two years my senior and we had lived opposite each other until I was eleven years old. Neither of us knew until that day that we each had joined one of the Forces. He was a soldier and astonished to see me in WAAF uniform. We chatted for as long as time permitted and when he learned that I was stationed in Shropshire he remarked, "That's strange, I'm being posted next week, I shall either be posted to somewhere quite close to you or to the South coast. If it's near you, shall we meet, Eileen?" There would have been nothing I would have liked better but the next letter from my father was to tell me that Reg had been posted to the South coast and within a week, like his sister and brother-in-law before him, he was dead. Like them he too had been bombed. My father later confided in me that his "Letting me go" as I had put it, was the best decision he had ever made, for he felt my safety was more assured each place I went to, than it would have been if I had remained at home. I told him that I was often very angry with some of the personnel who made stupid remarks like "This place needs a few bombs dropped on it to liven it up a bit," but luckily for me my war had few bombs. My losses were the partings from both men and women whom I had grown to love or like, as the case may be, and even the deaths of unknown men affected everyone, one moment a plane, the next a ball of fire. But my father was right, I was indeed very, very lucky.

If I had considered 1941 and 1942 as being exceptional in the way of constant change the remainder of 1943 made them pale into insignificance. Before I finally depart from Redcar there is one small memory I'd like to relate, because somehow I can never quite forget it. Even on a course we found ourselves committed to regarding Monday nights as the night we were confined to our Billets in order to make sure that we did any little outstanding jobs, such as sewing loose buttons on jackets and shirts, giving our black shoes a really good shine, insteps included and not least, shining up our bed spaces. On this course I always felt that this night belonged to our wee Scottie, Ruth. It was no doubt that her accent was so evocative of Mac — I was always a willing listener to everything she had to tell us in Room 5 — but it was her expression of "Get those stockings sorted, baby" which had me really puzzled, until she explained that it was just the Scottish form of "darn your stockings". Needless to say I left with that advice from Ruth signed into my autograph book.

But all things come to an end, even clerical courses, and soon I was back at Tern Hill. In next to no time I became so involved in picking up the threads there so that the course soon became lost in oblivion, but not for long. This time I was to become VIP in a very big way and for many different reasons.

CHAPTER TWELVE

OTHERWISE ENGAGED!

Ricky was posted on the 13th May and I reminded him of 'the sawdust incident on my first morning as an NCO' and had teased him that I would pen in his autograph book "I'm now off — early tea". In the end we compromised — he wrote those words in my book whilst I obliged by writing something more to his liking, in his, for which he gave me one of his beaming smiles.

Since the arrival of our new Squadron Leader I was now back in the General Office and a few weeks had elapsed when I found myself alone. Eileen was nowhere to be found and Bill was probably at Band Practice. The Squadron Leader opened the hatch and said that the Wing Commander needed some books which he, the Squadron Leader, had in his possession. Feeling a bit irked that I had no one else to deliver them, I told him that I would have to deliver them myself, which would mean leaving our office unmanned.

I got my cycle from the rear of the hangar and set off with the pile of books under my arm, but they were of assorted sizes and awkward and I barely managed to mount and get started when my front wheel ran off the concrete path and down I went, books, cycle, the lot. My cycle fell back on me and the books lay scattered around in all directions. Although I had heard the crack of my left elbow on the concrete I remember more clearly, my panic, as help seemed to appear from all directions.

"Are my knickers showing?" I kept asking repeatedly.

We were into August and the day was a warm one but rules had to be obeyed and so no one was allowed to move me until help arrived from Medical Quarters. I knew the Medical Corporal and remembered her more from the fact that a sister of mine had given birth to a daughter in the February before I enlisted and this Corporal had the same Christian name as the child was given.

Other than that none of us knew her very well as she was very much the introvert. After that morning I was to wish I had never known her at all.

When she arrived at the spot where I was lying she simply lifted my left arm and dropped it back without ceremony.

"Yes, it's gone, I'm afraid," was all she said. I was taken to Sick Bay, but I cannot remember what type of transport was used. I was very hot wearing my jacket and beginning to feel the pain but all I was offered was a stool to sit on. There was some paperwork going on but no attempt was made to bring me any relief, not even the removal of my jacket.

I finally realised why nothing was being done. There were two ambulances on camp but there was a rule that one of them must remain on the airfield at all times in case of there being a "prang". It seemed that the second one was out on duty. I sat on, feeling a little sick as the time passed and nothing changed. It was now a good two, or two and a half hours, since my arrival at Sick Bay and my being sat on this very uncomfortable stool. When I had left my Squadron Leader to take the books, I had called out to him "I'm just off, Sir, I'll be back in five minutes." Famous last words!

Suddenly and surprisingly he walked in on his way to lunch at the Officers' Mess with just the intention of enquiring as to how I had fared. When he saw me sitting on a stool I cannot express his anger. This quiet dignified man almost went berserk. He was given the information about the second ambulance and the staff added that they had even considered transporting me on the pillion of a motorcycle used by dispatch riders.

"Didn't anyone think of finding someone with a car?" he shouted. "Get something done at once." Things went from bad to worse for he next asked what I had been given by way of food and drink and when told nothing at all, he looked on the point of bursting a blood vessel.

I cannot complain of my treatment once I arrived at Cosford Hospital, where I noticed that even the rank of Corporal was regarded with some respect. Two things troubled me greatly during my stay. When it was found that my left elbow was dislocated and it had been put into first plaster and then a sling I took a walk up the ward. I had only ever been in a hospital as a visitor and found being a patient a different matter altogether.

It was then that I first blessed my rank of Corporal which allowed me to be in the bed nearest to the door and far away from the two WAAFs who had each undergone a tonsillectomy. They had little tubes protruding from their mouths and were making the most frightening gargling noises deep in their throats. They sounded as if they were about to expire at any moment.

The second mishap caused me to wish I was anywhere other than in the bed closest to the door, for it was both personal and very degrading to me. Each Sunday we were asked if we would like to join in the church service appropriate to our given religion, and since we were confined to our beds and therefore had no way of escape, even had we wanted to, I couldn't see we had any option.

I had had an enema only a short while before the service started and being in the bed nearest the door meant that I was also closest to the Padre holding the service. Sure enough the worst happened — far, far worse than that day way back in 1941, when I had only water to control. At last I could bear the situation no longer so I had to suffer the indignity of requesting a bedpan and screens to be put round my bed to hide me, but nothing could ease my embarrassment at the most appalling smell I was creating and worse still I could feel my bottom touching the contents of the bedpan. They finished the service without me, leaving me with my shame behind the curtains. After that things improved!

Once my arm was in a sling there was little point in keeping me in hospital very long — so I thought of the irony of my longing to come to Cosford nearly two and a half years ago, and now here I was, but my old flame had left long ago. I was not there long as it was decided that I should go to convalesce in a huge house one might easily have referred to as a mansion.

There was only one other WAAF who outwardly showed any sign of affliction and she shared the name of a well-known author, Phyllis Bentley. She had her right leg strapped up after an operation for cartilage. I went ahead and again was surprised to be greeted with the apologetic words "I am sorry, Corporal, you should, of course, have the privilege of having a bedroom to yourself, but I'm afraid we are rather full." I was ushered upstairs to a smallish room where an LACW was already standing beside her bed. We were introduced and it appeared that I was expected to go to bed, early as it was, and that my tea would arrive on a tray very soon.

One never realises how much one is incapacitated when having the use of only one arm but I was unprepared for the fuss which accompanied my being undressed, washed and having my teeth cleaned. What puzzled me was that the LACW appeared to be using some kind of sign language which I failed to grasp. She seemed to be very harassed and then suggested it would save time if she helped me to undress. Whatever her motive was it failed and it was just as I was getting into my bed that I suddenly became aware of the reason for her panic — I was getting into an apple-pie bed she had made me. I looked up and winked and when I was asked if I wouldn't feel better if I stretched myself out in my bed, I lied through my teeth.

"Oh, no," I said, "I always sleep curled up to rest my sling on my knees." Satisfied with this odd explanation the door was closed and we both split our sides with laughter.

"You are a brick, Corporal," said my new companion, "I never dreamed I would be joined by an NCO, they usually have a room to themselves — you won't put me on a charge, will you?"

"What after all those lies I told?" I said, and after that we got on fine. I was to spend three weeks there out of the five weeks I was absent from Tern Hill and, but for the pain, I must confess I would not have missed one day in the large, beautiful house.

It was not long before Phyllis joined me again and we fell into the habit we had used whilst in the hospital. She was given a walking stick to help her progress with walking and by strange chance, as it was her right knee which was gammy and my left arm, she would use her right hand to carry her stick and use my good right arm, so that we tagged along together in this way; she with her stick on the right, I with my arm in a sling on the left, whilst at the same time we became good buddies.

There proved to be a way Phyllis could help me as there was a passion for playing a card game called "Hearts", and handling cards with one gammy arm isn't too clever. The idea was that, within reason, any number could play and we had to pass the cards around in order to get rid of all the hearts we held in our hands. But there was a snag — if one got caught with the Queen of Spades one tried not to let the other players know because the player left with this deadly card in their hand scored ten debit points. I may not have remembered all the rules, in fact I did relearn the game after the war was over, then I forgot it once more. Hour after hour we sat beside the very imposing fireside and dealt these cards onto a round table. All went well until the nurse came at 9 p.m. one night to take a WAAF away who had suffered a mental breakdown. The rest of us were allowed up until 10 o'clock, our night drinks being brought well before that time.

On this particular night we were all as engrossed as ever when to our astonishment the WAAF who should by then have been fast asleep, walked along the beautifully balustraded landing. She was sleepwalking with her arms outstretched and was fast reaching the top of the magnificent stairs. We thought for a moment she was play-acting but she suddenly began to scream "I've got her again, I've got her again, the old black bitch." From that night the game was forbidden and we were told we must spend more time out of doors.

Walking through the shrubbery and trees one day we met up with a WAAF who surprised us by telling us she had brought the playing cards with her. There was no trouble in getting us to exercise after that, we just sat down on the grass or pine needles and played more than ever before.

There was one funny incident concerning Phyllis and myself worthy of a mention. Although supposedly ill, all of us fit enough had to attend church on Sunday mornings, and as we were both C of E, we hobbled in together behind the others. One Sunday Phyllis whispered to me as we passed the children seated in pews to the left of us, that they were the children from the nearby Doctor Barnardo's Home.

"Cor! look at those two — do you think they've been shot?" one young boy piped up, to the amusement of all within hearing distance.

My arm remained stiff and slow to respond to the daily physiotherapy and exercises, so the suggestion was mooted that, as I was a Clerk/GD my use of a typewriter might help to bring it down. When I went back to the Orderly Room at RAF Cosford this idea proved to be useless as I could not understand a word of Latin — and who can read doctors' writing anyway? But it was through my being sent back there that I became very VIP, because the morning of the 24th August dawned and with it my "coming of age", which in those days was one's twenty-first birthday. I did not mention this fact, after all there was only one other WAAF Sergeant or Corporal in the Medical Orderly Room and the day would pass like any other, I supposed, but how wrong I was proved to be.

About 11 o'clock I looked down the long office as the door opened and I gasped in amazement.

"Oh! Hello Sergeant," I said, as I recognised one of the staff from Tern Hill. "Whatever are you doing right down here so early?"

"Someone in the postal section thought that a certain Corporal belonging to us, but far away in Cosford Hospital, is having a very special day today," he grinned. "Look at all the keys and cards and then you have this special little box too. You're twenty-one today, aren't you?"

I asked if I might forget rank and give him a hug for coming so far and he laughed.

"A kiss would be better," he said.

The Orderly NCO had stood bemused but suddenly she sprang to life and offered me warmest congratulations — who but I, I wondered, would spend their twenty-first in an RAF hospital? The Sergeant left to return to Tern Hill with my request to thank the PO staff for both recognising my special mail and doing something about it.

I opened all the cards and silver boxes with keys in them. A lot were from home — they had done me proud, considering the difficulty of obtaining these in wartime. There were some from "Q" 's relations, his parents and a special aunt, whom I had visited on my own one leave, again arriving on a snowy night long ago. I had left the little box till last and was stunned when I saw what it contained. It had travelled all those thousands of miles from India, and here I stood on my twenty-first birthday looking at what must surely be intended as my engagement ring from "Q". It fitted me perfectly. That surely must rate as being exceptionally Incident Prone.

"Q" had never asked me if I would like to marry him, neither did he have any knowledge of what had happened before we met.

As for me, I suppose the whole day was heady. Being in hospital for this birthday was unusual enough in its own way and receiving all my mail because I had been at Tern Hill for two years and four months — long enough to be really well known. But the ring really was out of the blue because there was no letter with it, no proposal of marriage, and though I had always secretly known that "Q" could only ever be second best, I could not lightly dismiss his love for me nor his loyalty. Hadn't he told me so often and written as many times more? Mac had never remembered birthdays, so why should he remember this one after such a long silence? I packed up all my mail and placed the ring on my finger, it was useless pretending that I did not know that it signified his definite intentions.

It was but a few days to my learning that, at last, after a stay of five weeks, I was to return to Tern Hill. I went back wearing the ring and made a more-or-less formal announcement that I was now engaged to "Q". I wrote my letters of thanks home and made the same announcement to my family and told them how much I appreciated their generosity in finding me so many pretty keys and cards during wartime. My heart was not as light as it should have been but "Q" 's parents seemed more than happy with our news.

I thought again of my long journey up North and then the small train which bore me out across the moors in total darkness. I recalled his father, short but hardy, meeting me at the tiny railway station. "Q" would have been with me had it not been for his sudden promotion to Sergeant and subsequent posting to India. I had been the only passenger to alight from the train and I remembered well the crunch of our footsteps in the darkness as we struggled over the snow which had hardened to slippery ice.

Many things had surprised me when daylight came, but first I had been aware of the warmth of their welcome and the fact that they had given up their bedroom for me and how lost and lonely I had felt in their big bed, as I had lain there with my thoughts all jumbled up. The walls outside surprised me after Surrey. I had never seen fields without hedges and surrounded by walls made up of various-sized stones without being cemented together. His parents had treated me with such a great sense of propriety which they had so obviously instilled in their only son and which he had used towards me when we'd been alone that evening when our cycle ride had ended up with our being in the heather. I recalled how I had been put on a bus the first morning and made my way to his favourite aunt who had a small farm. The kitchen was warm and cosy and his aunt set about making her own lovely crusty bread and some scones as I sat and watched. She had buttered the scones whilst they were still hot with butter from the farm and they really were delicious. She had been easier to converse with than his parents, but it was obvious that they all doted on this only boy, not yet twenty-three, when I went up this first time.

I was nevertheless taken aback by the speed with which all the relations set to work embroidering pretty tablecloths and tray cloths for our bottom drawer — how could I not know after that, that this was my engagement ring.

When I arrived back at camp I made straight for what was left of my staff, now only Bill and Eileen. As I was about to turn the corner of our hangar I almost bumped into our new Squadron Leader coming the other way. What a retentive memory, I thought, for his first words were "A long five minutes, Corporal!"

"Yes, Sir, five weeks to be precise!" I grinned.

"Where are you off to now?" he enquired and I told him I was off to see my staff. Not that they deserved such loyalty — if just one of them had been there to walk down with the books my accident would never have happened. Being a man of few words I expected our conversation was at an end, but he continued. "You have not yet been to the Orderly Room, then?"

"No, not yet, I thought I'd pop in there on my way back to WAAF Quarters and then, if it is alright with you, Sir," I said, "I will report tomorrow morning to take up my duties as before?"

"So you have not learned the result of the clerical course you attended last month at Redcar?'' he said, and his words startled me.

"Oh! My goodness, so much has happened to me during the past five weeks that I truly had forgotten all about it. Has the result been promulgated yet, Sir?'' I asked.

He did not answer the question, but wore his enigmatic smile. "Well, I think you must have had a very enjoyable time by the sea. Let's just put it this way, when the POR with your result on it was promulgated it was edged with black borders round it.''

I had a queer sinking feeling, remembering the bitter remark overheard by Eileen about me before I went, but I stood my ground. "Well, that doesn't happen even for a death announcement, I should know, I did stencil some PORs in the Orderly Room. Is this your way of breaking it to me that I didn't even make forty marks to merit the bottom of a grade 'C' pass?'' I went on "I tried, I tried really hard, honestly I did, and I'm very sorry if I've let you all down so badly.''

When I arrived at the office I was quick to notice that I was asked about my health, my accident, even my engagement, but not a single mention of the course was made. So it was true then, and they were ashamed of me. I left feeling like a damp squib and made my way to HQ. I dreaded meeting my Sergeant and late mentor, my sorrow was as great for him as it was for myself.

I opened the door of P.3 and suddenly my whole world turned crazy. Sergeant jumped down from the dais and, seemingly forgetting all the decorum he had tried to instil into me, lifted me up in his arms and swung me round in the air. "Who's a clever girl, then?'' he was saying.

"Whatever has happened?'' I asked, by now thoroughly confused.

"I asked them not to tell you, I wanted to tell you myself, I knew you wouldn't let me down — you obtained a Grade A pass with 82.5%! The first male or female ever to do so on this station. Well done!'' At last he appeared to be finished but then added as an afterthought "Oh, yes, the Adjutant wishes to see you as soon as you find time to go down.''

My engagement had already faded into the background as I tried to grapple with this latest piece of really wizard news. I made my way down the stairs and knocked on the Adjutant's door with a feeling of *déjà vu* as I entered, and now for the first time in my life an Officer was rising to his feet and holding out his hand to me to offer me his congratulations.

"Well, Corporal Stapley, you've really done us proud this time, but then haven't you always? Ever since that long ago day when you were taken from the Cookhouse. I was on to Group one day and was told about the course you had attended and how exceptionally good the results were. I think they said that there were five Grade 'A' passes, anyway the most ever. I mentioned that we had an interest in the results as one of our WAAFs had attended. They checked and gave me the wonderful news that you were one of those who had obtained over the 80% required for an 'A' pass.''

I stood there wondering if I should thank him when I was suddenly assailed with a strong feeling that there was more to follow. "Is there some other news, then, Sir?" I found myself saying.

"Yes, I'm afraid so. I was told that we would not be able to keep you on strength here as you would be underemployed, or rather they felt you could be better employed elsewhere . . .''

So my two years and five months at Tern Hill had come to an end. I was three months off my nineteenth birthday when I had arrived on 16th April, 1941, and now I was barely a week or two past my twenty-first birthday. I had started work in the Cookhouse, had written my way into the elitist HQ, and then out of it into engineering. So many memories flooded my mind as I packed to leave; all my hitchhiking with Joy; the only time I had been volunteered to play Netball at nearby Shawbury as a poor substitute for someone sick; the young soldier at Hodnet who became my "Cavalier Unknown"; my day out in Shrewsbury with the Army Officer's wife — and I knew that one day I would return to the "Dingle" as I would never forget it; the wonderful lorry driver and his information on the oddity of the church at Ormskirk with both tower and spire. Now it was ended and I felt a little bereft as I said my goodbyes to start all over again.

CHAPTER THIRTEEN

WALES

I was on a train and leaving England to make my way round the North coast of Wales, passing through Rhyl, another of our long-distance hitches. It was a glorious day as the train bore me westwards. The sun made the sea sparkle till it almost dazzled my eyes. Still ringing in my ears were all the voices of those who had assured me that I would love being at RAF MONA on the Isle of Anglesey. So the journey progressed and I made my first crossing of the Menai Straits.

My arrival was daunting, to say the least. I struggled down an unmade sun-baked clay path toward a Nissen Hut which proclaimed itself to be the Guardroom, complete with full kit, gas mask and tin helmet. It was no joke after the way of life I had just left behind. Even less of a joke was the fact that the first person I met was the WAAF Commanding Officer.

"Ah," she greeted me, "you must be Corporal Stapley. I'm afraid we need you very badly, we are very short of WAAF NCOs." I put down most of my load and before a few more sentences had passed between us she added "I do hope you are not too tired as we need you to be Duty Corporal in the Guardroom tonight." Nothing like being thrown in at the deep end, I thought. All the same, I must admit I liked her direct approach to life, for she was both pleasant and easy going. As if Guardroom Duty was not enough, even worse was the fact that I would no longer enjoy the luxury of living in Married Quarters, the Nissen Huts reminding me all too vividly of my early days at the Training Depot.

When I did start work I was pleased to learn that I would once again be working in the small Orderly Room, always my favourite working place, and to my surprise I found I was to make up the staff of three. The male Sergeant would by my senior and then we had a young Welsh girl who hailed from Beaumaris, who had as yet only done five months' service. From the outset it was plain that rank meant nothing to her, but to be fair neither was she concerned that we called her by any Welsh name which came to mind. Sometimes she was Blodwyn, sometimes Megan and often one of the lesser known Welsh girls' names. She was as bright as a button, always chattering and always aware of the state of affairs. It was she who moved my desk so that I could look out on Snowdonia, the fact that the light was incorrect for typing was of small consequence in her eyes.

My first task in the evenings was to send cards to my family, friends, and most of all to Mac, with regard to my new address and the fact that my long spell in Shropshire had come to an end.

I made no bones about the fact that I was very unhappy with my lot. To be continually told that Snowdonia was beautiful when all I could see was a distant mountain, much smaller than I had anticipated and perpetually shrouded in mist or more often fog, with just a snowcap showing, made it all a nonsense to me. Each morning as I entered the OR, both the Sergeant and Blodwyn would ask "Have you unpacked yet, Corporal?" and I in reply would always tell them that, but for my personal photographs which were on my bedside table, a privilege extended to a Corporal, my kit remained in my kitbag.

After several days had passed Blodwyn had an idea which she hoped might cheer me up. "Can you do shorthand, Corporal?" she enquired, knowing full well that I couldn't. "Only with it being September the evening classes are about to begin in Holyhead and I thought you might like to come with me?"

"Well, why not?" I said and listened whilst she told me that a station bus left one evening each week and waited to bring us back.

We left after tea so that we travelled in twilight and returned in darkness. Whenever I was bored I tended to smoke a few extra cigarettes. I hated them so it was partly bravado to show I earned sufficient pay to be able to afford them. We made the mistake of sitting in the front row on our first evening and I learned nothing, nothing at all. Our tutor was a Welshman with an accent thick enough to cut with a knife. I gather shorthand is not a subject one can learn in a hurry in one's native tongue, but what should have sounded something like "Ay, Chay, Jay," sounded in Welsh pure gibberish to me. However, there was some light relief for I was totally fascinated by the tutor's constant calling of "You, Jones, there at the back," or if not Jones then Evans received similar corrective measure.

The weekend came and I was wondering how I could pass the day when I again met up with the WAAF Commanding Officer. "Are you wanting something to do, Corporal?'' she enquired, obviously aware of my apathy. ''I've just heard that my cycle is among those which have arrived at the railway station,'' — I wondered if my own cycle was there too — but she continued to suggest that I might like to take the bus into Llangefni at her expense, then on to the station to collect her cycle and ride it back.

I was very lucky weather-wise and set off in brilliant sunshine, but when I reached Llangefni I learned for the first time the strange routine concerning the buses. Passengers had to alight, watch the bus, still in sight, make a ''U'' turn, before returning to request the same passengers to board the same bus again. However, this seemed a small penalty to pay for having an afternoon out at my CO's expense, and the rest of the journey turned out to be quite pleasant.

On my arrival the atmosphere quickly changed. A solitary worker at the railway station, whom I approached with regard to the cycle, was blunt and that's putting it mildly. He pointed across the road where I became aware of a couple of shops or so, and nearer to the station a tangled heap of cycles tossed willy-nilly from which I was expected to find the correct one. I attempted to make some sort of appeal for help, but received what I expected, a few grunts and a reminder that there was a war on and he was the only one there. It was a long, hard struggle but I finally found the right bike and was delighted when the key to the chain lock worked immediately — but my luck ended there. One tyre was flat, nicking inner tubes I knew was the order of the times and replacements like gold dust.

''Try in the shop there, maybe you'll be lucky,'' the old man shouted across, but I had no luck and being depressed, wondered if he had sent me because he was plain cantankerous.

I was unsure of the mileage back to MONA. I guessed it to be about six, and set off on my trek. It was not a pleasant experience pushing a cycle with one wheel running on its rims and again I was on a road without pavements. At first neither of these factors bothered me greatly but after a while the sun vanished and I was surrounded by a mist which in no time seemed to turn to fog. Because Surrey is an inland county I had never realised how the geography of a place affected sudden changes of temperature and weather. I pushed on bravely but soon began to feel frightened with no pavements nor lights working on the cycle to guide me. The fog thickened and started to swirl around, confusing me, until my nerves became shot to pieces. When I had all but given up hope I turned to see if I had imagined that there were vehicle lights coming up behind me, the first I had seen during my long trudge.

To my dying day I shall always remember that post office van. I was in such a state that I thought it might be a mirage. How great my relief when it drew up and stopped beside me. I knew that many of the islanders spoke only their native Welsh but probably the war may have changed this to some degree. My postal driver was Welsh speaking but my situation was so obvious that we soon got the message across. I was still unprepared, however, for the next development. His van was one of the larger type with many sacks of mail and the necessary mesh protection inside. I was alarmed when he opened the doors, moved the sacks about until he had formed a kind of hideaway and then pushed me into it with the cycle on top of me and proceeded to cover us both up with mailbags. I had expected to sit up the front with him, but only then did he use his limited English to beg me to keep quiet and not to move as he would be stopping to pick up a colleague and later on stop again to put him off near his home. There was no further hitch for I could not move under the weight of the cycle and the mailbags, and my legs and feet soon became cramped. But what a "Gentleman of the Road" he turned out to be, for when we finally stopped I found he had gone out of his way to drop me outside the main entrance to the camp.

A hot bath and a good meal was all I longed for, but both had to wait until the WAAF CO had been given first-hand all the details of my adventure — or misadventure!

When the next night came during the following week for Megan and me to attend our shorthand class in Holyhead, I went a little more prepared. Firstly I made sure we got seats in the back row with the idea that, if we couldn't learn the subject, we could at least indulge ourselves with those rather swanky cigarettes, the Turkish ones called Passing Clouds, which were sold in pink packets and were oval in shape. They gave off a strong aroma and tended to make us drowsy, but in those days they were considered to be very elitist, so we just sat back and let the lesson drift over our heads.

I knew Holyhead was a port but I never once saw it, though we could hear the sailors coming ashore to buy drink and knew them to be foreign from the constant "Ja, Ja," which interspersed their speech. It was as we left the hall to make our way back to the station bus that we suffered an unnerving experience. Blackout was being strictly adhered to, but the light from a pub door showed up a huge sailor standing bang in the centre of the pavement, legs astride, in what looked like a very menacing attitude. I whispered to my young Welsh companion.

"Don't ask any questions, just do what I tell you." She got the message and came and took my hand but I shook it off and told her to continue to walk toward him as if we were going to remain side by side, then on the order to run, we would confuse him by dividing up to run either side of him. The pub door was closed so we were now in total darkness but I gave her a sudden push, urging her to run and not to stop until we reached the bus. It worked and we were safe, but once on the bus we both vowed we would never attend the classes again. In view of ensuing events our words were to prove to be very prophetic!

I must have been there for three or four weeks and was still very unhappy, worsened by the fact that as well as being confined to our Billets for the usual Monday night we were also confined a second time in a week. It appears that some undergarment had been found in very unpleasant circumstances and of course no WAAF would own up to having had a "sexy night", nor to its ownership. I was furious that this ugly incident might spoil my hitherto unblemished record, but as we were confined *en bloc* this did not happen.

What happened next was simply incredible to me. When you waken each morning unhappy and expect it to be just another day you are totally unprepared for your life to change dramatically, just as mine was about to do. The last big day had been back in 1941 when I was awakened to learn that I was to leave the Station Cookhouse and to work in HQ. Well, this was to be another such event. Luckily I had arrived in the OR before Blodwyn and found the Sergeant had opened all the mail as usual, sifting out the trivia before taking the important mail into the CO. He was standing up reading a letter with great intensity.

"Good morning, have you unpacked yet, Corporal?" he said, turning to me to give me my usual greeting.

"Oh, don't start that again," I said. He then handed me the letter marked 'Confidential'.

"No, I don't want you to," he said and urged me to quickly read the letter before our little Welsh girl arrived.

"For goodness sake, don't mention its contents to her," he added.

Even after I had read it through twice I was still stunned by the short succinct matter it contained. Finally I spoke. "But surely, Sergeant, this does not include me. I've only been here at most a month — it says a skeleton staff will remain so surely I will be included in that?"

"It means exactly what it says. We are all moving to Scotland and as you are on the permanent staff that includes you."

"Well, it won't take me long to pack," I quipped and Sergeant smiled.

"To think of all those mornings we have hinted that by now you should have settled down and unpacked and now I am begging you not to do so.''

At that moment Blodwyn arrived, chirpy as ever, completely unaware that her life was to change so soon as she was to remain at MONA. Her chatter was difficult to parry that day and I was saddened when she suggested that now we had given up our shorthand classes she had been wondering if there was any possibility of our being off duty on the same day as she would like to take me to her home in Beaumaris to meet her parents. Sadly, it was a pleasure I was to miss and when the day of departure came I realised I would miss her too, but was thankful that she would always be one of life's survivors. For some inexplicable reason I never again smoked Passing Clouds cigarettes!

CHAPTER FOURTEEN

SCOTLAND

If the word "Workaholic" had been in vogue then it would surely have applied to me. I revelled in my work. There certainly had been no physical passion in any sense, not so much as a date. From the time I had left in June to attend the clerical course in Redcar, I had been constantly on the move. Back to Tern Hill, followed quickly by my spell in Cosford Hospital and the convalescent home; again my return to Tern Hill and now, when it was still only about late September, I was about to leave for Scotland after my surprisingly short stay on the Isle of Anglesey.

After we had been given official notice of our pending move I set to and once again sent postcards relating my news and change of address and I suppose my family and friends were as startled as I had been that first morning when I had read the letter. I doubted if "Q" had received my first letter in India — but no one could say I was not being patriotic with my war going from England to Wales and now on to Scotland all in the course of just over a month. I had only my Irish Christian name of Eileen to offer the Irish, but later even this matter was to be corrected in a very unusual way.

One fact only remains clearly in my memory. I sent my postcard to Mac and I can well remember the very words I wrote — "You can forget about Wales — would you believe I have been posted to 'Your beloved Scotland'?" Because we travelled up *en masse* the journey left little impression on me. There was food and a lot of chatter, and for me that was that.

Well, at least it was a change, but in more ways than I was to bargain for. Firstly, there was a large personnel there already, which tended to make us feel somewhat second class. This was to apply especially to me as I was to find out later. The WAAF Quarters were in the very beautiful, large Dunragit House, so important that it is to be seen on maps of the Galloway area. It was about three miles from the actual camp of Castle Kennedy, which in turn was nearer to Stranraer. It was staffed by an Admin Corporal and both kitchen and cleaning staff remained there permanently as we were allowed to spend our days off there and apply for a meal in advance as the small NAAFI only opened in the evenings.

The rest of us boarded a lorry or trucks, but Roll Call was taken first, either in the hall or outside in the drive, depending on the weather. We were then transported to Castle Kennedy for breakfast after which we dispersed to our respective duties. When we boarded the transport our cycles were thrown up on top of us. We needed these, as the Messes and NAAFI were on one side of the road leading to Stranraer, whilst the main part of the station was on the other side. Only those who worked in the Cookhouses, did cleaning, or were NAAFI staff, were left behind.

This was the only RAF Station which had a small facility for Corporals of either sex, too small to be termed a NAAFI but very welcome in its way.

Depressed already by the fact that we felt second-class personnel, for me personally there were two more disappointments in store. My greatest disappointment was when I discovered there was no vacancy for a WAAF Corporal in HQ Orderly Room and since I had already done quite a stint on Engineering it was to this section I found myself allocated. Equally depressing, I found that five WAAF Corporals shared room 20 in the lovely house, but I was once again to be in charge (i/c) of one of the Nissen Huts, tucked out of sight from both the house and the very long drive set in woodland.

I was pleased that many of my girls had come up from MONA with me and I must add that they were a grand bunch. Here the Corporals were allowed to have their respective beds facing lengthways down each hut, thus affording us small alcoves and a table on which to place our personal belongings, mainly photographs.

When we had time to get acclimatised we found there was sufficient decent weather left to make it possible for us to cycle down to Luce Bay, where we would throw off our uniforms. We wore shorts underneath our skirts and so just replaced our shirt with either a blouse or jumper. Here we had some high jinks running along the shore among the sand dunes. Only occasionally did we use the back drive to reach the sea because it was a much longer cycle ride. At last I began to notice the importance of my "Grade A" pass for I swear no WAAF Corporal ever took Roll Call more often than I. Although I was not the sporty type, I never had any complaints to make to do with Roll Calls or marching. In fact the other Corporals and the girls were all most complimentary.

"This Corporal knows what she's doing. No waiting about when she's on — you are either there or left behind!" they would say. It was true — I had them Roll Called with great speed, then aboard the transport for the day with their cycles thrown up behind and we were off.

I felt it was a real come-down when I found I was to work for only one Engineering Officer. As he was a Flying Officer, I thought that he was the lowest rank of Officer I had worked for so far since leaving HQ Orderly Room at Tern Hill.

A noisy babble greeted me from the end room of the Nissen Hut, which was to have been my place of work. I did my best, I really did, but finally I went along the passage to see the Flying Officer. He was a Canadian, who was called "Rocky" for that reason but also because his name was Rochester. He was young, married and lived with his Canadian wife in a house in the beautiful grounds of Castle Kennedy. He was very easy going and the moment I explained that there was no way that I could work in that small, stuffy, overcrowded office, he promptly told me that I could use the empty office opposite his own. The outlook was just a clay bank with brambles growing on it, but there were two telephones wired up. I accepted and workwise it proved to be a good move as it saved me from constantly trudging up and down the corridor.

The staff in the office appeared to be workshy, so I'm afraid with my speedy attitude to life, I tended to leave them to fend for themselves; but they were kind enough to make sure that I was aware when the NAAFI van drew up and always came along and said "Tea and a wad, Corporal?"

There was one other pleasant fact which followed me to Scotland and which surprised and pleased me greatly. Although, as I've mentioned, I was not up front when it came to sports, my love of and great ability to march well still held me in good stead. Well, I must admit, I almost lost the privilege of leading the WAAF Squad on a special big parade, for we were marching to the bagpipes which I found very novel and almost thrilling. It was when it was suggested that I should twirl the baton, or however the Scots describe this activity, that I jibbed and told them that surely with all the Scottish lassies around there must be one who could achieve this feat. I'm pleased to say I got my way and no one was more proud than I was as we marched past the hangar and around part of the perimeter track. I've loved the bagpipes ever since.

My friendships were limited as naturally the Corporals billeted up in the big house tended to look to each other for company and rarely used the Corporals' small room on the camp. So I spent most of my evenings with my girls in our hut and got to know each of them very well. Life was busier and my apathy soon passed. Although my Flying Officer always referred to me as Corporal, he soon said "For Goodness Sake, Corporal, don't be so stuffy, call me 'Rocky' when in the office!" This is not to say that I did not know each of the other Corporals and where they were employed and I was on first name terms with some of them.

I had been in Scotland for about five weeks when I decided one day that the telephonist Corporal had blown her lid. The two telephones on my desk were always ringing, so I was staggered when I picked one up and she said "Eileen, there's a call for you."

"So?" I said. "Why don't you just put it through as usual?"

"I don't think you understand," she went on, "this is an outside call and whoever is calling you believed you would be in HQ Orderly Room." She paused, then added, "There's something else unusual about this call . . ."

"There certainly is," I interrupted, "I don't know anyone in Scotland and I haven't had a date since I arrived."

She went on to tell me that she was not certain whether it was a Scot who had lost some of his native tongue, or an Englishman who had picked up some of the local accent.

"It's a man, then!" I said. "How interesting, best put him through and we'll find out what this is all about." I picked up my other telephone. "Hello, Corporal Stapley speaking," I said, rather warily.

A voice, "larded with the Scottish accent" spoke softly. "So you've got yoursen a decent posting at last."

My heart almost stopped beating. "Mac! Oh, Mac! Where are you? What a fantastic surprise!" I could hear the laughter bubble up in his own voice as he strove to hang on to his soft burr as he replied "At hame with my mither, where every good Scot should be." (I pray the Scots forgive my attempt.) If we did not know we were in love and always had been anyone listening to our bantering that day would have had no difficulty in guessing, for we were both as high as kites! But an even greater surprise was in store for me when he next spoke.

"When are you coming up for the day? Can you get Wednesday or Thursday off?"

"For you, any day," I answered.

It was not a spur of the moment thing, he had times of trains from Stranraer to Ayr all planned and said he would meet me on Ayr Railway Station. Both of us seemed loath to stop speaking. I can see myself still, shut all alone in that little office with just a small window looking out on my brambles, forgetting everything, even the engagement ring on my finger — Mac was back in my life and I was struggling against calling him "Darling" when that was the only word I wanted to say.

How I got through the hours until it was time for my departure was sheer torture. I must have found someone willing to run me into Stranraer by transport and because I was such a workaholic there was never any trouble when I wanted time off, I was just happy to work with my hands and my brain.

I'm almost certain that I went up on a Wednesday and I can recall that day just as if it was yesterday. It was another beautiful autumnal day. Until then Scotland was only "Dunragit House", the main camp and its cinema, the lovely hours spent among the sand dunes down on the shore, or wandering round the old ruins of Castle Kennedy, ivy covered and with some of the most beautiful gardens I have ever seen. But now, with my ring in my pocket, I was travelling up to be with "My Mac". Even if he wasn't going to ask me to marry him, I couldn't bear that he should know that I wasn't free — I felt deep in my heart that he would have been shattered if he had known the truth and I did not want it otherwise myself, anyway . . .

Always there was the sea and the sun and here I was again making another coastal trip up through Girvan and seeing Ailsa Craig amid the sparkling water for the first time. I was bursting with happiness and felt I could have walked on the water.

The train was slowing down and pulling into Ayr Station — soon, oh! very soon I would be with my Mac again. I looked out of the window and my impression was that the platform was very, very long. It was not only long — but bare. There was no sign of Mac waiting for me anywhere. I had a return ticket but there was a war on so no porter in sight, indeed the platform was empty but for a man in civilian clothes away in the distance, looking up the line seemingly waiting for the "Down" train.

Where could he be? Maybe he had been held up. Perhaps I should go out as I had a ticket to see if he was on his way. I began walking up the platform and was about to pass the man wearing civvies when I nearly jumped out of my skin. Mac, teasing me as always, turned round quickly. "Boo!" he shouted.

"Oh, Mac," I said, laughing. "Don't you ever do that to me again." How prophetic some of our words turn out to be.

I had never seen him out of uniform and I was amazed that for today, at least, he was no longer my lovely Brylcreem lad. His hair, newly washed, was lighter than I had ever seen it; the soft breeze blew it and I noticed it was wavy. I may not have been different that day, though I suspect I was, but looking back I can clearly see that Mac certainly was. He was on a 'high' for him, he laughed more but teased as much. When he had telephoned me I had tried a little teasing myself by telling him that I would be well outside of the thirty-mile radius.

"Well, that's never bothered you before," was all he said. But the hours were few and precious and I was forty-nine miles from Castle Kennedy, plus any mileage we might add on.

It may sound foolish now, but I fell in love with Ayr right from the start. Mac had kissed me as of old and held my hand as if he would never let go of it and it was in this fashion that we made our way from Ayr Railway Station to the town. Neither of us asked where the other had been nor what we had been doing and as always I left him to do the navigating whilst I was content to take in every detail, bubbling away as usual.

"Oh, look Mac," I exclaimed, "The Tam-O'-Shanter Inn, how romantic!" As we progressed so I enthused over each new Scottish delight. I wanted to linger but was amused when Mac, knowing nothing about my gaining a Grade "A" pass said, "Come on old Sassenach, you need educating." I knew for certain when he uttered his next words, that they were definitely very unreserved for him, for this gentlest of men, who had never uttered one wrong word in all the times we had been together and all the lovely hours we had shared said surprisingly "A tea and a pee and off we go" — he just had to be on a high to say something like that.

So we did just that, found a tearoom in town, after which I discovered that being educated meant our going to Alloway, the birthplace and museum of his national poet, Rabbie Burns. We got on buses and we got off buses but the journey left no memory with me, just Mac and I holding hands and me listening to his enthusiasm as he made the visit come alive for me. I am certain, well, almost certain, that I signed the Visitors' Book as we left. After we had seen everything we made our way out through the turnstile and I found myself gently ushered along until I was standing under the thatched eaves above the porch. Mac took a minute camera from his suit pocket and crossed the main road to take a small photograph of me standing there in my greatcoat, for by now it was the end of October, or more probably early November.

I remember how I remarked that we were lucky he had some film in his camera on this auspicious occasion and I watched him putting his tiny camera back in the pocket of his suit as he recrossed the road.

"And where am I to be taken, Sir, for my further education?" I said cheekily, when he reached me. Just a silly, nonsense question, but I little guessed that those words of mine were to be prophetic too. His next words took my breath away. Here stood this beautiful young man of twenty-five and a half years old and I now three months or so past my twenty-first birthday — a woman — not the young girl of less than nineteen and a very "rookie" WAAF when we had first met. My whole life had been centered around him, even during his long silences, and I knew he was finding it difficult to accept, not just my quick changes of rank, but that I was no longer a young girl. Yet still I was stunned when he took both of my wrists in his hands and looked me full in the face.

"I'd like to take you home to meet my mother," he said and I stood there lost for words, for I can say in all honesty that such a thought had never even entered my head.

"But Mac, I'm a Sassenach, whatever will she think about that?" I said foolishly.

He smiled, still holding me gently by my wrists. "She will be very, very disappointed, because she is waiting on us going," he replied.

I am telling you the way it was on that far-off day — for only time yields up its secrets. It was as if we had changed roles. For once Mac was the chatterbox, whilst I no longer looked out of bus windows but at our hands clasped on our laps.

"I never thought the day would dawn when I would see you look so shy," I recall him remarking.

"I'm not shy, Mac, really I'm not, but I must admit I am a little nervous."

We made the journey back to Ayr, changed buses and walked up a very long unmade country road to reach his home, but I was unaware of any of this. All I recall was our arrival and his mother waiting to greet us.

CHAPTER FIFTEEN

MAC'S MOTHER

The house appeared to be the lodge to a very large house and estate. I knew his father had been a shepherd at the time of his birth, but as I only met his mother that day I went on erroneously believing that his father had become a Ghillie — to the unenlightened English, I thought it was the equivalent to being a caretaker or keeper of an estate, and so it followed on that I imagined that his mother had been allowed to remain in the lodge after his death.

His mother was no longer young but I sensed immediately the great affinity between mother and son. Although I think my nervousness had been due, in part, by my thinking that his mother might resent there being another woman in her son's life, in no time at all I felt as if I was being embraced into it too. I knew immediately from whom my Mac had inherited his gentle character but spiced through with a sense of wit and humour.

I had already discovered that Scots, to my way of thinking, are usually good cooks, so I enjoyed the home-made griddle scones and all the other offerings not usually found in Southern England. After our meal we sat for a time chatting.

"Jimmy, don't you think Eileen might enjoy a walk round the estate before it gets too chilly?" his mother said. My hand flew to my mouth and I could not stop myself.

"Oh! My God! Forgive me please? Of course, you have a name, and here I am calling you Mac in front of your mother. I have never heard him called by any other name." They were both amused by my distress.

As we were about to leave the house to climb the steps leading from the back of it to see the beautiful view from the hill top, Jimmy asked his mother if she needed her coat as it was already getting a bit chilly, but she declined. We climbed up quite a long way until we reached a stile behind which was a small summerhouse. It was too hazy to see the sea in the far distance so at first I did not think anything of the fact that his mother suddenly said "I think I've changed my mind about my coat," and Jimmy returned to get it. There was so little time that she could not prevent her ploy becoming obvious to me. She used my name easily, as if she had said it many times before.

"What goes on between you and Jimmy, Eileen? It's now well into the third year since you met. He talks about you all the time when he is at home and when he thinks he has said your name too often he doesn't fool me when he refers to you as 'Old Sassenach'. He uses it more as a term of endearment, so you see, you need not be embarrassed that you call him Mac."

"Oh, no, you've got it all wrong," I said with great urgency. "He made it quite clear to me soon after we met in the spring of 1941 that he has no intention of marrying me."

"But did you know that you are the first and only girl he has ever brought home in his life and that is why today is very special to him? Did he actually say those words to you?"

"Oh, no, he never says much at all, does he? It was the postcards he sent me postmarked Ayr 1941 — each of them had a cryptic message." We were speaking very quickly for she was puzzled and wanted to know what these messages were that her son sent on an open postcard to tell me that marriage was not in the offing. I told her that both were Mabel Lucy Attwell cards and that the first was a picture of a young woman with her knitting all tangled up and covering her lap — I did a lot of knitting in those days — and underneath was the message "Portrait of an English Lady — never saying die".

"Goodness, whatever did you read into that?" his mother asked. I said I thought that he was telling me that I was chasing after him and wouldn't give up, but she negated that suggestion and I went on to tell her that the second card was much more to the point. It bore a picture of two babies at each end of their respective cots and this time the message read "Marriage old chap — it's not a word, it's a SENTENCE".

"And do you think my Jimmy went into Ayr to look out those postcards especially to tell you in such a way?" she chuckled. "What about the studio portrait of himself, it took much courage on his part to overcome his reserve to have that taken especially for you? I saw his message written on it 'Lots of Love, Mac,' and if he wrote it he meant it. That was when I first guessed that there was someone very special in his life."

Then she said two more things that made no sense to me at the time, but over which I was to ponder often in the future, "He will not speak for you, he thinks you are so very young and what if he doesn't come back?'' He was climbing the grassy hill in the distance so I had no more time to question these surprising statements — after all hadn't we been apart many times and hadn't there always been his long periods of silence, so why was his mother saying these things to me? Some sixth sense told me that she longed to say more but for some reason she was holding it back. Of one thing I was now certain, she had no doubts about me, she had accepted that we three were together as if that was the way it should be.

"I've brought the camera back with me," announced Jimmy and proceeded to use up the film. There were just three more small pictures left, so he took two of me sitting on the stile with his mother, now wearing her coat, standing beside me. The second one was from a different angle and took in the wee summerhouse in the background. I was not wearing my greatcoat but I was wearing my service issue woollen gloves. He then handed me the camera and sat himself on the stile.

"Oh, Mac," I said, slipping back to his old familiar name, "you know how hopeless I am at anything mechanical and I'm not used to seeing you with your hair all a-blowing without any Brylcreem," but I shot it for better or worse, and in the event it was worse, for I later wrote underneath my copy "Mac — but I nearly didn't get him" for he was almost on the edge of the shot. It was such a happy snapshot, he looked so content, with his broad smile and his hair as I had never seen it before.

Back in the house, with all my wants attended to, we were all dreading the moment of departure.

"May I ask one favour, please, before I leave?" I suddenly asked Mrs Mac. "I have both read and heard about the beds built into the thick walls of this type of house and think you might well have one behind those curtains. I would dearly love to see it, if that is not being too impertinent?"

She laughingly drew back a curtain to reveal the neatly-made double bed.

"Oh, how cosy it looks!" I remarked. "I almost wish I could snuggle down in it and stay the night," and both Mac and his mother burst into hearty laughter. I went on to thank her very much for satisfying my curiosity.

"I hope you didn't think me rude?" I said.

But the hour of departure had come and we could delay no longer. She held me close to her in a light but warm embrace as if she had known me for a long, long, time — so I hugged her too. We both found words inadequate so we said very little at all — what

was there to say after the niceties? I did not want to leave her, especially standing there all alone. I did not want this day to end — and long afterwards, as I was passing Ailsa Craig on my return train journey I thought, I do have a song to remember all this by —
"This Is My Lovely Day —
this is The Day I shall remember the Day I'm Dying,
They Can't Take This Away —
it will be always Mine, the Sun and the Wine — the Seagulls Crying."

First we had that long trudge back down the unmade country road, all of one and a half to two miles, then a bus to Ayr Station. Mac, who was now Jimmy, or James, as I preferred, was giving me his tender, gentle kiss as the train arrived to bear me back to Stranraer and then on to Castle Kennedy. A new man with a new name, maybe, but not to me! Three people had met, lived, laughed and eaten together that day, yet we each held a secret in our hearts. Mine was the engagement ring from "Q" which was in one of my breast pockets. Mrs Mac had been torn apart by hers, for she had longed to tell me something but she had made a promise not to do so to her son, the secret he himself held.

Mrs Mac had got as close as she had dared but it was to take many years for the full truth of this day to yield up its secrets and many, many more for the full story of this and the days that followed it, to be revealed. But should this get into print and there are sufficient readers of it who want to know what happened to the three of us from here on, then I shall write a shorter book and it will be entitled *"Mission for Mac"*.

For now I can only take you with me and tell you that copies of the small photos taken that day arrived quite soon but, as usual, there was no letter. It was some time before I realised that for the first time since we had met, Mac had not given me any address.

I wondered if I should write to his mother, but his documents were no longer where I was stationed in Scotland, so I did not have an address for her either. I began to think that perhaps I had been right after all and that his mother was probably romanticising, as Olive used to do over her Stanley. I was bitterly disappointed, but being officially engaged left me without the right to share my heartache with anyone else, even had I wanted to.

CHAPTER SIXTEEN

WILMSLOW

When one moves from one RAF Station to another it is the usual practice to get as much new kit as possible from the stores and when I left Tern Hill I had been the proud possessor of a new pair of shoes. It was soon after I'd been to Ayr that I discovered they were missing from my bed space. I was very angry because I have always been the type of person with "would-be perfectionist tendencies" and so I have an innate loathing of dishonesty. When I went to the WAAF Commanding Officer to report their loss I let off steam about our huts having to remain unlocked for sudden inspections, thus affording us no protection against such misfortunes as this. She listened earnestly and I thought I had made my point, but was hopping mad when I discovered her sympathy did not extend to my having them replaced, rather a certain sum would be deducted from my pay until the missing shoes were paid for. My girls in our hut were absolutely furious.

It was wintertime now and we sat huddled round the fire in the centre of the hut and for some strange reason I can recall the yarn one of the WAAFs was spinning. Before enlisting, it seems she had worked some place where they packed sanitary towels. One day a young lad came in and idly picked one up and asked what it was for. We all went into hoots of laughter when she told us that she had explained to him that they were chin warmers and how she had put one on and put the loops around her ears!

It was a night for humour — one of the girls returned to the hut absolutely doubled up with laughter, so much so that she could hardly speak.

"You'll never guess in a million years what's happened, Corporal?" she at last managed to get out. "Today five pairs of shoes have gone adrift and one pair was the CO's taken from the house." I couldn't refrain from having a chuckle myself.

When I went into work on the main camp the next day I went to enquire if the information was true, and if so, would all the other five losers be treated as I had been. Actually, only one stoppage had been made by then, but I felt a principle was at stake. To be fair our WAAF Commanding Officer smiled as she said "We called in our own Service Police and later the Civil Police, you will probably be refunded your reduction next payday!"

I was, and the culprit was caught. He was one of the men employed to cut down some trees and he had been stealing them to sell in Civvy Street.

My thoughts of Mac were never far away and as Christmas and Hogmanay approached I was excited at the prospect of being in Scotland for these festivities. I even wondered if he might come home as he always had in the past, but alas, that was something I was never to know. My hopes were dashed when I learned that I was being sent back to England for the whole of the Festive season.

Once one has attended a course it appears that the powers that be have a penchant for testing one with another course, just in case one's first good result was a fluke. My second clerical course was at Wilmslow, Cheshire. Strangely enough, I cannot bring this course to mind as readily as my one at Redcar, perhaps it was partly due to my disappointment at going at that time of year, or maybe because it was wintertime and no nearby sea. I worked hard and made many friends and as far as I remember I got another good pass mark, but I cannot remember whether it was another Grade "A".

My main recollection is of the notice which went up the night before we were due to finish, stating that all WAAFs of NCO rank were permitted to leave overnight. I was surprised when one of the Corporals approached me and asked if I would like to go up to Manchester with her. I did not know her very well but she suggested we would stay at the YWCA which she assured me was in St Peter's Square, then go to a cinema.

We had not been paid for three weeks, so though I realised I'd be well on my way back to Scotland, I thought it a bit reckless with regard to cash. Nevertheless, the idea did appeal to me, though I cannot even recall this Corporal's name. I little guessed this was going to be one of my VIP adventures!

We intended to go straight to the YWCA by bus and make sure of booking us each a bed, I think the bed plus breakfast was only 1s/6d (7½p), but nothing went right from the start. It was unusual for me to find myself not in command of any situation, but I sat on the bus with my new companion and we waited and waited and waited. No one came, neither driver nor conductor and even more weird to me, no passengers came either.

"Oh, come on," I said. "Surely you've made a mistake?"

"Anything goes in wartime," was her only comment as we got off the bus. Suddenly she asked me to pool my small resources with hers to see if we could afford a taxi. She reached the conclusion that we could, with enough left over for our night at St Peter's Square. I love things to run on oiled wheels and was apprehensive as she raised her hand to hail a passing taxi, something I had never done in my young life.

It was one of the older type models. We got into the back and I was surprised when she left the driver to cope with both sets of complete kit, which one always had to take on any course.

"Don't worry," she told me, "that's his job and what we are paying him for." So I watched as the poor man struggled to place it all on the front platform, next to where he would sit to drive the taxi. These last weeks had left me edgy and restless and this strange and hurried situation was not to my liking. I felt I could not cope, but at last we were off.

We both fell to chattering about the course, then about our respective stations. Youth always has so much to say and do! After a while my anxiety returned.

"Aren't we going a long way?" I asked. "We won't have enough money to pay him at this rate." No sooner had I made this comment than the taxi drew to a halt and my companion was soon out on the pavement waiting for the driver to lift our kits off the platform. She started to chatter again whilst I was watching and wondering what the driver was doing on the far side of the taxi. He appeared to be messing about with the headlight. Then, to my horror, he got back in the driving seat and was off. Remembering the loss of my shoes I now felt this was the big one and we were both about to lose all the kit we both possessed. I grabbed the other Corporal's hand.

"For God's Sake, we'll have to run after him," I yelled and we started to chase after him along the pavement, each of us shouting at the tops of our voices, though the street was totally bare.

"After him, after him, stop him, thief, thief!" Just when we thought the worst had happened, the taxi stopped as quickly as it had sped off. Breathless, we were unable to speak.

"What the hell happened to you two?" asked the taxi driver, much to our amazement. "One moment I was adjusting my headlamp, which needed dipping, so I chose to do it at the lights, and the next I got in and started up. It was when I realized that your chattering had ceased and I was left with a deadly silence, I turned round and found my vehicle empty.''

"Sorry," we both at last managed to say, "we thought you had reached the YWCA, so we just got out on the pavement waiting for our kit, when to our astonishment we saw you fading away in the distance.'' We all had a good laugh, but I'm afraid that was all I saw of Manchester. We found we could afford some supper, probably fish and chips, and I even had sufficient cash left to get myself and my luggage by taxi to the railway station the next morning. From there I would start my return journey to Scotland, another January was here again, the January of 1944, but Hogmanay was past!

CHAPTER SEVENTEEN

RETURN TO SCOTLAND

There was nothing significant about this journey. As far as I was concerned I was just travelling all alone from A to B. It was just another dull, dreary day and I was looking forward to being back and getting settled into the hut once more. It was early afternoon when I arrived and I knew the small NAAFI we had in the grounds of "Dunragit" house would not yet be open. Indeed it was a dull time of day all round. I made my way to the hut, still unlocked even after the stolen shoes affair, and thought how lovely it would be to throw off my kit, tin helmet and gas mask and just lie on my bed until the girls returned from work to light a fire and put some life into the hut. If only life was as simple as that!

When I opened the hut door I received the shock of my life — I had nearly all my kit with me but my bed was barren. All my personal photographs were no longer in my small alcove, my whole bed space was bare, everything I treasured had disappeared. I was really choked and just sat down on the bare springs of my bed and burst into tears. The hut was very cold and I was both weary and hungry and desperately in need of a good hot cup of tea. Perhaps I should go up to the house and seek the latter, I thought, but with my tears, inertia had set in, so I sat alone and wept tears of bitterness.

It was thus I was sitting when the hut door was opened and the Admin Corporal entered. "Oh! So you're back then, how did you get on this time?" she enquired. Before I could answer she became aware of my sorry state. "Please, don't cry, we never gave a thought about it being a shock to you. Cheer up I have some very good news for you. Whilst you were away in Wilmslow on your course, one of the WAAF Corporals from the house was posted. As you know there are always five Corporals in the largest room, so the remaining four had a vote as to whom we would most like to be our fifth roommate — no other name was mentioned, we all voted for you with one accord. This will make you happy when I tell you that the reasons given were that you are always smartly dressed, quick, lively and able to handle the girls. We took if for granted that you would approve, so I've had all your personal belongings taken up to room 20 in the house and they are beside your bed. Come on, let's go up to the kitchen for some tea!''

The Admin Corporal was a Scot and there were two Marys, one a Scot, the other English, so to differentiate between them the Scottish one was always called Mary Mac. She, like me, was also a Clerk/General Duties and worked in Flying Control, so came into contact with all the flying personnel. The fourth Corporal was a tiny Jewess named Betty, but she ended up by being called ''Yiddisher Momma''.

For me ''Sassenach'' became the order of the day. Only my Mac had ever called me Sassenach way back on that seemingly far-off day last autumn, when he, a Scot, had found me in his ''Beloved Scotland'' whilst he remained in my native England. That was one of things I found so comforting in wartime; there we all were, a mishmash of people of differing nationalities, yet we all enjoyed breaking down the barriers just by using silly names to which none of us took offence. In fact, though my new colleagues did not know it, ''Sassenach'' was bitter sweet to me. Now that Mac had disappeared, seemingly for good this time, it was soon accepted that I was the WAAF Corporal who was engaged to a Sergeant who was serving in India.

Dorothy, the Admin Corporal, was very tall and, to the WAAFs in general, very awesome. I quickly found the reason I had been allocated the bed nearest to hers. I can't recall one morning through those dark wintry days when she did not rise about 5 a.m. and make a start on her *toilette!* On went the light and, though she was quiet, I was disturbed from that time on. Her skin was so beautiful that it looked like alabaster. Every part of her face received so much care that not even one eyelash was out of place once she had applied her mascara. Atop all this her hair, slightly browner than blonde, really shone. I suspected that the girls felt nervous in her presence but we all loved her just the way she was and accepted her with ease.

Only once I remember her making a comment on my hasty make-up procedure. She was right of course, for haven't I told you that I always considered my nose my worst feature.

One morning she sat on her bed watching me. ''No wonder your face looks a mess. Every morning you fly straight to your nose with your face cream, then some powder, and occasionally you actually get around to plucking your eyebrows.''

''Ah, yes,'' I replied, ''but aren't you all glad when someone is needed to do the blasted Roll Call.'' They all laughed and said ''Point taken,'' and the subject was never mentioned again. Actually, I'm being somewhat hard on myself, my hair was my crowning glory and the envy of most of the girls, and my nails I managed to keep tastefully short but well polished, even when I had cause to help out with the typing.

Luckily, paywise, all our duties fell into the Grade 4 categories of Administration, Accounts, Clerk/General Duties and so on, but as Dorothy stayed in the house to supervise the staff in her administrative role, we four went into the camp each day. Mary Mac and I became really close by virtue of our both being clerks but also because I was still on engineering. We would cycle back from the Mess together after breakfast, pick each other up for lunch and again at tea time until it became quite an established routine. I had to turn off right before she cycled toward the Flying Control Tower. Actually, this was to bring about quite an hilarious situation. It was on a day when I had been up in the house for about four months and for some reason I cannot recall, Betty had to go to Flying Control too, so there were three of us instead of the usual two.

When Mary Mac and I were alone, usually a bit late, I would turn off right without dismounting and call back over my shoulder ''Cheers for now,'' which I meant to imply that I would be on the corner when the next meal time came round. I suppose, because there were three of us, it was why we decided to dismount. To my utter astonishment Mary Mac said ''These Sassenachs are queer, every day when we arrive here, Eileen dashes off to the right and calls back ''Chase me now!''

Just supposing Betty had not joined us that day, would Mary Mac, I wonder, have remained blissfully ignorant of a Sassenach's way of bidding her a temporary farewell?

CHAPTER EIGHTEEN

MARY MAC'S PLANS

The spring came and so did "Q" 's letters from India, but nothing from my beloved Mac. As I said, my colleagues just accepted the present situation because they knew nothing of my past and likewise I knew about their personal lives, as much as each wanted the others to know. To be fair we did all hold each other in great respect where privacy was concerned, after all we were all NCOs and that made for decorum also.

But a day arrived when Mary Mac asked Betty and I to join her, well out of bounds, as she wanted to visit Robert, who worked as a draughtsman on the ships at Greenock. So we all got the same day off and joined her. As we were booking out someone begged me to post a letter as soon as I was able.

We went by train and presumably Betty and I would have left Mary Mac with her fiancé so that they could have some time together on their own. We all eventually met up, late as usual, and began to run down Sauchiehall Street when I suddenly remembered the unposted letter in my pocket. I slowed down to look for a postal box, whilst all the time being urged to leave it until later or we would miss the train. I spotted a box and popped the letter in it. When I looked ahead the other two were doubled up with laughter. Both, like me, out of breath from running, they finally managed to tell me that I had just popped the letter in the night safe of a bank.

I noticed Mary Mac was carrying a net bag and being a true Sassenach I had not the least idea that Scots carry their lobsters, cooked or uncooked, around in this fashion. We caught the train and I watched as she threw it up on the rack above our heads, and from then on all seemed to be plain sailing.

Because my bed was the one nearest the door, it proved useful on many occasions so it came as no surprise to me when Mary Mac used it to open her prized possession on. I watched as she removed

107

the net bag and started to open the newspaper surrounding the lobster. There was no fancy wrapping in wartime. I reeled back in horror and the others were not amused at first; Mary Mac had taken the wrong bag from the rack and we now all stared at the blue-looking uncooked lobster writhing about.

"Wonder what the person who owns this will think," said Mary Mac, "when she reaches her destination to find her lobster well and truly cooked?" Here was where our Admin Corporal came in useful for she took it to the kitchen and asked the staff to cook it, so we did eventually have a lovely lobster supper. Yes! To be a Corporal was far and away the best rank for a WAAF to hold. Sergeants were thin on the ground, but we could always rustle up a Corporal to cover any emergency from Dental and Medical appointments, Cookhouse supplies, telephone calls, leave passes and often the police would need the odd favour, so we were well and truly buttoned up all round.

However, Mary Mac did cause me some distress when it was decided that I should make the long haul by train from Stranraer to Farnham, via Waterloo Station, for a week's leave. What with the cold weather and the strenuous weeks I had recently endured I was feeling at low ebb and in need of a good rest. I was even suffering with a severe headache, a malady unusual for me. I wondered whether such a lengthy journey was worth all the effort but finally decided to go.

It was not until I arrived with my small brown fibre case and quite a lot of uniform, tin helmet and gas mask that I found Mary Mac had fixed me up with a travelling partner. Still working for "Rocky" in the Engineering Department I was not as up-to-date with regards to other would-be travellers, as I would have been had I been on my favourite old Orderly Room duty. I went into the small Corporal's room and learned that she had made arrangements for me to travel with a male companion. He had a reputation for being a womaniser, but to add to this indiscretion on Mary Mac's part, I discovered he was totally kitted up as he was going home on Embarkation leave. I snapped at Mary, telling her that this was the last straw. How dare she make plans for me when I had a headache and would have preferred to travel alone!

She was immediately contrite and suggested taking me into Stranraer, where she would treat me to a meal thus saving me having to eat with my unwanted travelling companion. After supper I had to meet him at the railway station, and if Crewe Station was considered to be a nightmare, this one at Stranraer was far worse. To ensure getting a seat on the train, which left at 22.00 hours, it was necessary to be there by a quarter to nine. This was because the boat train arriving from Northern Ireland made the whole place one of tension as it was always swarming with RAF Red Caps (Police) — and I can only put this and my poor state of health as being reasons for my doing a most stupid thing.

As we both passed through the barrier heavily loaded I let myself be talked into handing "X" my leave pass and travel warrant. He was on the side of the Ticket Collector so he showed both his and mine and we proceeded ahead until we found a porter. We enquired which was the train due for London. To the surprise of both he pointed to one standing right beside us, completely empty of passengers. We dumped all our kit and "X" opened the door and started bundling the huge pile aboard the train, throwing our gas masks and tin hats up on the rack. He asked me if I was quite sure about not wanting anything to eat, and then, before I could stop him, he quickly took off his cap, threw it back on the seat and slammed the door. "I won't be long," he called back, "I'll just get a bite, a cup of tea and some cigarettes."

By the time I managed to get the train window opened to remind him he was capless and would be at the mercy of the Red Caps, he had disappeared.

For such a busy railway station a sense of eeriness prevailed, as I sat there all alone, so I stood up and reached down a book from my kitbag to read. Quite some time seemed to have elapsed and I began to get fidgety, fearing "X" may have been picked up. No sooner had this thought assailed me, than I found myself puzzled by another, for, to my utter astonishment, the train started moving. At first it moved only slowly so I surmised it was being shunted into a siding to make more room, due to the length of time before departure. But no! Suddenly it picked up speed and my heart started beating rapidly at this unexpected turn of events. The faster it went the more my panic grew as I realised the full implication of my situation.

Here I was, a WAAF Corporal without any documentation to prove who I was. "X" 's cap lay on the seat beside me — I had two sets of kit and he had two sets of leave passes and travel warrants. I kept wondering what he would do when he arrived back and found both the train and me in it gone. I wondered too, if I should pull the communication cord but was too scared to do so.

After travelling in this fashion several miles I suddenly heard the sliding door to the next compartment being opened. My feelings were mixed when two American Officers looked in at me.

"Good God!" one exclaimed. "Look who we have here — whoever are you?"

It was difficult to know where to start to explain but I made an effort and all went well until my lack of documentation came up. "Oh! Come on," I said, "surely you can see that there are two sets of equipment here — here is the cap he threw back on the seat when he left to go for food, a cup of tea and cigarettes."

They sat opposite me taking in my scared look. "Well, you'd make a darned young and pretty spy," they jokingly remarked. It was then that one of them noticed the bracelet Joy's mother had given me, way, way back in time it seemed now, and leaning forward read aloud "Eileen".

It does show my WAAF Number on the reverse side," I said, "but Eileen is all that it has on the front."

He immediately burst into the Yankee song "I left my heart at the Stage Door Canteen, I left it there with a girl named Eileen." This was the correct version of that song and it always irked me when Vera Lynn used the name "Irene".

"You are scared, aren't you?" one of them remarked and when I agreed I was and that I had a severe headache they proffered chewing gum which I refused and barley sugar which I accepted. They chatted for a while and reached the conclusion that they could at least tell me that I was, by accident they presumed, the only female passenger on an American Troop Train and decided that one Officer would remain with me whilst the other went up front to inform their Commanding Officer.

It was a nightmare. Soon the word went all along the train. I found myself with their CO and now there were three other Officers all as amazed as I was at my plight. With the familiar ease of most Americans each was now calling me "Eileen" and then the CO decided he ought to reach the train driver and ask if he had any suggestions for getting me out of my dilemma.

"Please, don't worry," he said when he returned. "It was the porter's fault, not yours — it has been decided that the train driver will request to make a short, unscheduled stop at Dumfries, where you must be prepared to get off as quickly as possible. My men will help you with all the kit."

I sat back for a while feeling slightly more at ease when I suddenly realised that I had no idea as to whether the train I should have been on would be stopping there. However, we soon reached Dumfries and the train drew to a halt. There was quite a hustle as many hands grasped various pieces of equipment and dumped them on the platform all to the shout of many voices and heads peering out of all the windows shouting my name. Satisfied at last that everything was in order, I could hardly believe my ears when I was ordered by the CO to lift everything back onto the train again.

Back once again and seated as before I heard one of the GIs say "That was a good tip you gave the driver to do that." I was in such a state that for a while I didn't realise he was joking.

The Commanding Officer spoke next. "I see you are engaged to be married," he said and I thought he was getting a bit personal. I wondered what this had to do with the situation. "The train driver has been instructed to put you off at Carlisle," he continued. "In fact no train is usually given permission to stop unless a relative is involved."

I had begun to follow his drift. "But you've made a mistake," I said. "I am not engaged to the Corporal with whom I was travelling." What a mess it all was and Mary Mac had got me into it. I was wearing "Q" 's engagement ring, but still deep in my heart I was as much in love as ever with my long-lost Mac. Now it had been decided for the sake of formality I would have to acknowledge "X" as being my fiancé to save any bother at Carlisle, where he would be waiting for me with my leave pass and travel warrant. This new turn of events left me so emotional that I did not know whether to laugh or cry!

At last Carlisle was reached and once again all the kit was lifted out of the train and the same heads were looking out all along the train as the CO and his fellow officers bade me farewell and wished me luck for the rest of my journey. With my biggest problem solved, now one nearly as gigantic faced me — how was I to get so much kit across the bridge which spanned the railway lines? The greatest care was being taken so that "X" was not allowed to come through the barrier. I had cause to thank a High-Ranking Army Officer, who, noticing my plight asked no questions, but simply and quickly lifted most of it for me and together we reached the other side. A railway official asked "Is this your fiancé?" and I nodded my head so he let me through to where "X" stood, capless, but not nearly as fraught as I expected him to be.

Of course, the train waiting for us was full to capacity, not a seat to be had anywhere, in total contrast to the way we had expected to travel when we had arrived so early at Stranraer.

That night is one best forgotten. We travelled all the way to London jam-packed in a corridor, sitting on our kitbags and with the remainder of our kit pressed so tightly against us that even a catnap was impossible. On top of this discomforture were the frequent comings and goings of passengers seeking the toilets in total darkness. I was no longer the happy, young eighteen-year-old who could fall asleep at the drop of a hat. I did my best to keep cheerful for "X" 's sake, after all he would not be returning to

Scotland after his leave, but would report to his place of departure for overseas. Nevertheless, I realised too late that I had been far too soft-hearted when he used this as an excuse to invite me to a London cinema matinee before crossing over to Waterloo. He lived South of the Thames and I well remember where, but will simply say near Croydon.

I was totally shattered already and then the film turned out to be a weepy and I am ashamed to admit that proved to be my final disaster point. Tired out, I at first started to weep softly, but when he reached to hold my hand to calm me, I became hysterical for the first time in my life and began to weep and giggle all at the same time and in no time I lost complete control. I kept begging for us to leave but "X" wanted to stick it out. However, even he was forced to realise that the cinema was filled with fairly elderly women all trying to gain some respite from the war raging round us and so, after an immense amount of being requested to hush, we collected our kits from the foyer and "X" had to prop me up as I was as weak as a kitten. We said our final "Goodbye", knowing we would probably never set eyes on each other again, and I caught my now familiar train home, but never confessed anything beyond telling them that I had caught an American Troop Train and had had to endure many problems. I made no mention of the visit to a cinema and my hysterical behaviour.

CHAPTER NINETEEN

THE PROJECT

When I returned to Castle Kennedy things were much the same as when I had left, but there was a real hint of the spring coming and I continued to work for "Rocky" as before and on 2nd April, 1944, I was completing my first three years in the WAAF. What happened next I can only tell you as I saw it through my own eyes and how I felt inside. How my actions might affect others, or theirs affect me, I could not know, and after three completed years I have to confess that a certain naiveté still clung to me. What I did, I did because I thought it was right at the time and I did not do anything lightly or willy-nilly.

It began one sunny afternoon when I returned and went into "Rocky" 's office to await his arrival back from the Officers' Mess. I have a vivid recollection of standing by his small window which, unlike mine, looked toward the hangars, and as I did so I experienced a feeling of *déjà vu* as I noted the dust and dead flies on his windowsill. I made a mental note to send someone along to clean up, then as I looked up I saw him approaching. He was always pale at the best of times, but as soon as he entered his office I noticed his face was ashen. He appeared to be choked.

"Whatever has happened?" I queried when I noticed a tear in each eye and immediately feared the worst. "Has there been a prang?" I asked, but he simply shook his head. "Did you go home for lunch? Is Mrs Rochester OK?" When it became obvious that he needed time to restore himself to his usual easy-going equilibrium I suggested he might be better seated and I would pop along the corridor and have someone make some tea.

This had an immediate effect on him. "No, please don't go — it concerns you." By now I was at a complete loss and could not think of one solitary reason that would bring about this state of affairs.

"Well, come on," I said. "What is this dreadful news that has upset you so?"

H

I was stunned when he replied "I am losing you."

"Losing me, what are you talking about? Please don't tell me that I am being posted yet again?"

"No, you are not leaving the Station, just me. It's that Bloody Grade "A" pass of yours. Of course, I've known all along that you've been underemployed, but I never expected you would leave me for the reason I am about to tell you. I was in the Mess standing on the fringe of the CO and other top-ranked Officers who were having quite a powwow. The CO spotted me and said, 'There's the answer, Rochester has the ideal WAAF suited to the task working for him — she's just shown her mettle on her second clerical course and could easily help him with the project.' "

I butted in to ask "But where am I going and what am I going to do and most of all who is the 'him' referred to?" Could I but turn the clock back to that surprising day, but alas, the decision was neither Rocky's nor mine.

"There is a project being set up on Command from Group HQ, apparently they have reached the conclusion that too many man-hours are either wasted or unaccounted for. A young FO has arrived and will commence the project tomorrow but it will be a marathon task," Rocky went on. "So it has been decided that you will work with him on that. You are to be allocated an office on your side of the passage, but down nearer the door, so you see, you won't even be leaving the building."

"Well, that's not too bad," I said, trying to cheer him up. "I shall still be around, and who knows, when the project is finished maybe I'll work for you again."

He picked up his telephone and rang his wife. I was sliding out of the door to give him privacy but he lifted his hand and made a gesture for me to remain. I heard his wife laugh and say "There you are, I've always said you love Eileen as much as you love me."

I was so horrified that I unthinkingly took his telephone from his hand. "Oh, Mrs Rochester, you know I only work for him."

She laughed and replied, "Well, you must confess that he likes you a lot, but seriously, I do hope you will come round to our home after working hours."

"Thank you," I said, "I'll try," though the invitation surprised me as I had never visited their home and could not envisage my doing so in the future. I more or less dismissed it as being a polite gesture on Mrs Rochester's part.

Office hours began at 08.30 hours, so I cycled my usual route the next morning and was surprised to see Rocky at his desk through the wide open door.

"Better this morning?" I joked and then turned into the office opposite to collect the few items I had kept there. The trestle table ran the length of it, so that the window had been behind me and when I left all that remained was this table, a filing cabinet, a typewriter and the two telephones. If just losing my services was proving tough to Rocky, how about my heart? I knew that would be forever locked into this small office — the office where the voice of my Mac had come through so surprisingly all those months ago. Nowhere on that camp would be such a shrine to me as this small office, I thought, as I took a last look out at my brambles. Closing the door I wondered if I would ever work here again, but I think I knew that I never would.

I made the short walk along the corridor and knocked on the door of the office I had been instructed to report to. When I opened the door I found myself totally unprepared for the sight that met my eyes. Here the trestle table ran across the width of the room and this, plus two chairs and one filing cabinet was all that it contained.

I was used to sparseness, but no one had prepared me for my first meeting with the tall, fair, curly-haired young Flying Officer who was seated facing the door. How often I had seen the then young Stewart Granger in films, yet except for his fair colouring and blue eyes, here sat an Officer who could easily pass for his double. Later I was to learn that there were many people who saw the great likeness and many years later when people saw photographs of him they made similar comments. We made the usual noises one makes upon first greetings and I was instructed to sit in the vacant chair opposite him, with my back to the door. The narrow table meant our working very close to each other and I noticed he already had some drawing paper unfurled on which, I suppose, we would be drawing up our charts. His first question threw me.

"Can you use a slide rule?" he asked and I promptly went into one of my inferiority spells. Just as quickly I decided that, if I was to work with him closely for some long while, I might as well act as a fully-fledged Clerk/GD.

"No, I hear you've been to Cambridge so such an item is quite normal for use where you are concerned, but I think I might well be able to race up a column of figures just as quickly as you!"

We were not to collect the man-hour figures from each section of the station — these were to be the responsibility of someone in the section. They were either telephoned in each morning — with regard to the previous day — or were brought to our office. It was no easy task, no job ever is when so many different people are responsible for supplying the figures that only the two of us would compile. Many a morning we found ourselves without several sectional reports. We were both quick; he with his slide rule, and I adjusting myself to my new clerical duties. Yet there was about him an easy-going manner so that at times he appeared to be almost teasing at life. It was decided immediately that we would take our lunch hour from 13.00 hours to 14.00 hours and close and lock the office.

Because every section on the station was involved, the news of my new job was soon known to all and I unwittingly became an even better known NCO than before. I seemed to be of particular interest to the other four Corporals with whom I was billeted in the house. I was used to being subservient to anyone of a higher rank, especially Officers, and I can now see with hindsight that had I questioned more and accepted less, the disaster that was to befall me might well have been avoided. Why did I not wonder why this young Officer, on whom many hundreds of pounds had already been spent so that he might be trained as a pilot and able to sport his "Wings", was grounded and doing what must surely be to him a humdrum task? I was intelligent yet still too naive to question anything I felt was truly no concern of mine.

CHAPTER TWENTY

INCIDENTS AND ACCIDENTS

During the first few days he made several comments, starting on my wearing an engagement ring and asking who "the lucky man" was and where was he stationed. He appeared to be somewhat taken aback when I told him "Q" was in India.

His next comment was personal and very pleasing. "I see you keep your nails looking beautiful and elegantly polished for wartime. Don't you find the use of a typewriter plays havoc with them?"

"Since I became an NCO I have, in the main, always had someone to do my typing," I replied, not able to resist having a slight dig.

Because we both had our cycles I did, for a while, cease to meet up with Mary Mac on our special corner, but we did endeavour to meet for a chat in the Corporals' room near the Mess on the other side of the road. After I had been working with F/O Duncan for some time I felt I ought to accept a few dates so that I could feel a sense of freedom from working with him in such close proximity. He did not appear to have associated himself with any of his fellow Officers.

A young and very handsome airman asked me if I fancied a long cycle ride to Newton Stewart, which he reckoned would be about twenty-five miles each way. He would pick me up at the bottom of the front drive to "Dunragit". How well I was to recall that ride and his remarking that we would work up an appetite for the meal he had in mind. He took me to a house there, where an enterprising housewife had given over her front room so that it held four or five small tables. The food was good, and I found her griddle scones evocative of those I had shared with Mac and his mother. So far, so good.

It was still early afternoon, so when my companion suggested we take a walk up over the mixture of heather and dead bracken to see the view, I agreed. But the whole day was spoilt for me for in next to no time he made his early advances to me. He had brought some form of protection which made me aware that he had come with such thoughts in mind. I was shocked but very quickly struggled free and started marching back on my own to where we had left our cycles. He offered no apology and we mounted our cycles and barely spoke a word on our return journey. I knew his name then but I have no wish to commit it to paper, in fact I did not try to commit it to memory nor to ever see him again. Lest I make myself sound like too much of a goody-goody, I must just add that I simply did not expect a comparative stranger to make sexual advances towards me.

In the early days when I had returned to camp on a station bus or truck from dances in Market Drayton I had enjoyed joining in when we parodied Anne Shelton's song of "Jealousy" and sang our own naughty version:

> "It was all over my SOP,
> My crime was my blind SOP.
> For he was an Officer in the RAF
> And I was a poor little innocent WAAF.
> He gave all his passion to me
> And now I'm a Mother-to-be.
> The heartache I cost him,
> No wonder I lost him —
> It was all over my SOP."

So my idea of accepting dates was ended as soon as it began.

It was one morning in early May, 1944, that a tragedy occurred far away about which I knew nothing, nor was I to learn for another thirty-four years. I woke up, lived through that day without the slightest feeling that anything was amiss, or that life would never, could never, be the same again.

A little while before I had shared in a traumatic day at Castle Kennedy. The whole station was alerted to the fact that the Commanding Officer ordered a complete "Attack Drill". As we had not been troubled by bombing he probably thought we might all be getting a bit blasé . . . Well, no one could deny that he could be right in that respect. Unfortunately, when the chosen day arrived it was one with more than the proverbial "Scotch Mist" to enshroud us, it bordered on being quite a fog. I learned from Mary Mac that there were those in Flying Control who were of the opinion that it ought to be cancelled, but no countermand was given so the Operation went ahead.

As soon as the Alert sounded Mary Mac and I met up in a dugout nearby, though we did not go fully inside, as we would have done had it been the real thing. She asked me for a cigarette as she had left hers behind in her haste, but I did not have any with me either.

As we stood in the damp, cold air from the entrance I heard her call out to someone running by. "Have you got a fag on you, please? I've left mine behind."

One of the pilots stopped and reached into his flying suit and threw her a packet of ten. Because of her job she knew most of the aircrew and they knew her. "That's all I have just now, take what you want," this one called out. "I'll see you back in Flying Control when I get down."

"Thank you," she called back. "Have a good trip."

A short while later we heard the terrifying bang and then the explosion.

"My God!" said Mary. "Someone's caught a packet." We knew we dared not move until the "All Clear" sounded, so in addition to our coldness, we now found ourselves shivering with fear. At last we were free and I found myself holding Mary's hand and running with her, with no thought in my head of returning to my own office. When we were told I held her in my arms as she burst into tears.

"And I've still got his cigarettes in my hand . . ." she said, over and over again. Yes, he was the one who had not flown high enough to miss the Black Galloway Hills, and though I had not known him I too wept tears of sadness for both of them.

CHAPTER TWENTY-ONE

ALAN

Although Alan and I had been on first name terms for some time I could not bring myself to ask him if he had flown that morning — I think I knew deep down that he had not. Yet again I let the opportunity slip by and did not question what a fully-trained pilot was doing working on a ground project. It was obvious that he had been grounded but I never once asked him why.

It was about this time that he asked me if I would like to meet him after work for a drink, a meal, or just a ride on our cycles. I said I would think about it, after all I was engaged and "Q" 's letters arrived from India with great regularity. But there hung about me a deep sadness, a feeling of unfulfilment, so that after a while I succumbed and we went, sometimes doing one thing, then another until with time we had done all three.

I loved the time down on the beaches best and found him to be an avid photographer with an excellent camera, but even this in its way I found daunting for I have always been unphotogenic. Nevertheless, so many snaps were taken that just a few had to be OK. There are photos of me wearing his civvy trousers and hat making me look quite cheeky, another of me lying on the cliffs high above the sea at Portpatrick, my chevrons showing on my sleeves and my hat and his camera case lying beside me as I slept in the sun. He took some incredible shots in the beautiful gardens at Castle Kennedy of waterfalls, trellis bridges and pools with huge water lilies. Some photos had me in them and there was a mere handful which I had attempted to take of him at his request. He was gorgeous to look at and so photogenic, with his curly hair showing as he pushed back his cap at a rakish angle.

I knew it couldn't last but the reasons why not were twofold. As soon as I had agreed to stop living like a nun, as he put it, and join him in a little harmless fun, he began to pester me to stop wearing my engagement ring. I was with him all day, every day, our hands only a few inches apart over the trestle table, yet for a while I kept reminding him that the other person, whom he had never met, was also involved. I would stress how much "Q" loved me and I knew that to be true.

"But you don't love him really deeply, do you?" he was quick to notice and remark.

"There is a matter of honour," I responded. "He is so far away and can do nothing about the situation himself, which isn't really fair at all, is it?"

But like most things, the decision, when it was finally reached, was made for totally different reasons. We were having dinner in "The Auld King's Arms" in Stranraer one night, which was totally out of bounds to other ranks, when in walked my WAAF Commanding Officer with an escort. I blushed furiously and kicked Alan under the table.

"Now look what you have made me do," I said through gritted teeth. "For over three years I've obeyed regulations almost to the letter, and now I find myself in all kinds of misdemeanors and I don't like it. I don't like it at all, in fact I bloody well hate it!" We could hardly get up and walk out but whilst I was finding it difficult to sit the meal out and eat, he just sat there nonchalantly and maddeningly unconcerned. He was quite a bit younger than me, but because he was so tall and strikingly good looking he appeared to be older than he was. That night I told him that I did not feel I could honestly live with myself whilst wearing "Q" 's ring and I took it off.

I was waiting for the call from my Commanding Officer the next morning and feeling resentful that Alan had asked me and I had allowed myself to get into such a reckless situation.

The morning passed without incident but Rocky was late back after lunch and as he passed the door of our office he opened it and popped his head in. "Have you a minute or two to spare me, please, Corporal?"

I got up and followed him along the corridor and into his office. He came straight to the point by telling me that he was late back because he had been home to see his wife.

"I understand that your WAAF CO was displeased to find you dining out in Stranraer with F/O Duncan. She is not alone in being distressed by your sudden change of lifestyle, after all you were not selected for the project on your work alone, but because we all believed you to be a model of discretion in all other aspects of your behaviour. She feels that, since I got to know you quite well before his arrival, you might prefer a gentle reminder from me. The reason for my going home was to discuss the situation with my wife and she begged me to remind you of her offer to visit our home — you can bring Duncan with you, or not, as you please, but at least it will give you breathing space to think where you want to go from here.''

"Oh, Rocky," I said. "What a very nice man you are, I would dearly love to take up the offer. Alan must make his own decision, but meanwhile please tell Mrs Rochester that I shall be more than pleased to accept any invitation she is prepared to offer.''

When I returned to tell Alan of this sudden and unexpected turn of events he irked me by accepting the news with his usual nonchalant attitude. Having made no male contacts as far as I knew, I realised he would expect to come with me. On the other hand I did feel him to be somewhat insensitive about the part he had played that had brought about this necessity for using the Rochester's private home as a bolt hole from prying eyes.

The visits started immediately for, as Rocky's wife pointed out, very tactfully I thought, there were many days and hours when she found herself alone. I was made to feel at home and they seemed to disregard my lowly rank, yet I never abused those visits by calling Rocky's wife anything other than Mrs Rochester. To this day I have never recalled her Christian name, even though I must have heard it used often. On the surface all appeared well as far as Alan was concerned, yet some sixth sense made me wonder why this young ex-public school and Cambridge educated handsome Officer did not receive quite the same warmth of welcome. I found it easy to shrug off because I was young and Alan was such a happy extrovert and like most Arien characters had the need to have some excitement astir. He was very likeable and if he had any flaws I failed to see what they were. I did worry quite a bit that he often refused to listen to me when I suggested that time was flying and that I would be late booking in — those perfectionist tendencies of mine, he called them.

We were at the Rochesters' home for supper on D-day, 6th June, 1944, and as Alan had his camera with him as usual I have some very good snapshots taken that evening. There are one or two with Rocky and his wife and a really good one of Rocky with his wife on one arm and me on the other — my engagement finger is clearly visible and bare. It seems no one took a photograph of Alan that evening. Even when we did not go to the house, and of course, such an arrangement would have been an intrusion on their marriage, we still went into the grounds and spent many happy hours there. There was so much to see — I just loved looking at the huge water lilies and the multicoloured rhododendrons. Sometimes I would sprawl on the grass as I listened to the constant clicking of Alan's camera nearby. Here at least I felt that our meetings, innocent enough by anyone's standards, were not giving cause for complaint. We rarely sat down together on the grass as we had all day to chat whilst we were working.

Now I found it was my nights which were troubling me. Those same "perfectionist tendencies" as Alan referred to them, were torturing me with guilt. The thought of breaking the news to "Q" was a decision I still had to make. Deep down I knew that Alan's only attraction for me was the fact that he was always with me and he was so very handsome and always urging me to live for the day. But what of "Q" so very far away and so obviously very much in love with me? It never entered my head to play around as other women and girls did — to me there was black and there was white, but no grey in between. So the letter was finally written and dispatched to India, but I was not very proud of myself. I was even less proud when a letter arrived for me from the North of England. It was one of the most bitter letters I have ever received, requesting me to return "Q" 's ring to his home plus the many embroidered tablecloths, napkins, etc. I took it for granted that the letter had been penned by his parents — many years were to pass before I learned of my mistake. It had been written by an aunt I had not met on my visits, so I was at least left with some happy memories of his parents and the aunt I had visited on her farm, recalling the smell of her lovely home baking.

I had worn the ring all those months believing that Indian gold wasn't hallmarked and yet surprised by the fact that mine had been. How different my decision might have been had I magnified it and read the inscription " 'Q' to Eileen 24.8.43" , the date I had received it on my twenty-first birthday. How I came to get it back and discover this fact quite accidently, I am not yet prepared to divulge. I suppose poor "Q" was just as utterly staggered when he realised that I had not seen his intended message of proposal — I can only say that to learn so late in life that two men had truly loved me makes truth of the saying that "Youth is wasted on the young."

With my boats burned, Alan wasted no time in taking me to Leominster for a day out and when I returned I was wearing the ring he bought me there. It was not gold this time but platinum with a diamond in the centre and, oddly enough, a zircon either side of it. Zircons sparkle so and Alan admitted it was as much as he could afford. To me it was an odd assortment pricewise, but being a Virgoan, a sign of the quick and busy people, the zircons' sparkle seemed to befit the variety associated with the sign.

It was soon after this that he asked me to get a weekend pass so that we could go to stay in the huge hotel which stands high on the cliffs at Portpatrick. This was another favourite place of ours and one we had cycled to quite often, so that we were aware of the many moods of the sea and the spiky rocks sticking out of it. There are also many little sandy inlets where, during the war at least, one could sit for hours without seeing another soul, but to go for a weekend, I told Alan, just wasn't on. Why I said that I do not know, for I had spent many hours in many sheltered places alone with him and never once had cause to think of him as other than an honourable man. To my astonishment he picked up the telephone, requested an outside line and proceeded to book two single rooms in our own names and not even on the same floor.

I was a bit anxious when he knocked on my bedroom door and feared the worst, but no, he simply chatted for a while, kissed me "Good night" and returned to his own room.

On one of the afternoons when we stretched ourselves out on the grassy slopes below the hotel I was astonished when he suddenly remarked, "For a WAAF Corporal as much in demand for her favours as you are, it's really quite startling, because when one looks at you closely, do you know you do not possess one really good feature?" He ran through them each in turn, my eyebrows needed plucking and my eyelashes were too short. My cheekbones were too broad and my nose nothing more than a piece of putty stuck onto my face. "Of course, you have very beautiful hair when you are allowed to drop it from its ribbon and the bow to your lips is shapely," he conceded. Worse still, the sun shone on a few light hairs on my chin and he touched them and said "We must get some attention for those."

I felt totally shattered. "Are you quite sure that you want to marry a girl with so many defects? — and that is only my face!"

Just before we left for Castle Kennedy he was up to his tricks again and we went down to the shops which seemed to be cosily snuggled in the harbour. I was amazed to find that he had purchased a very cheap wedding ring, the sort of trinket one purchases when on a trip to the seaside. When I tried it on it fitted me perfectly and for a while I believed he had just bought it for the size I would need sometime in the future. But outside of the shop he begged me to wear it back to camp to shock the other Corporals into believing we had really slept together.

"Oh, come on, Al," I said. "Mud sticks, you know, and they are probably thinking that already." I never quite saw how young and really childish he was, but I went along with his idea of a joke. Of course, they didn't believe the worst — they knew me too well for that — but thought we had quietly sneaked off and got married! I had a devil of a job getting them to believe that nothing had happened, nothing at all.

There have been many times when I wished myself standing on the grassy sward near the hotel. One rare sunny day Alan had pointed out the blur of distant land and told me we were looking at Northern Ireland, which he believed to be about seventeen miles away. In retrospect I can clearly hear the sounds of the rough sea and the eerie wail of the foghorns and slipping from my bed that night so long ago, seeing the flashings from the lighthouse. These, however, were not to remain happy memories.

There is another shore, of another land, one I have never seen and wonder if I ever shall! But back to the summer of 1944.

I cannot remember much about the actual "Time and Motion" study, which is what I suppose it was. I do have the faint recollection of being amused by the fact that we were even expected to record the time personnel spent in the toilets.

CHAPTER TWENTY-TWO

BANNED!

All my life I have wondered why none of the men I met ever felt it necessary to ask me if I would like to marry them, let alone do them the honour. So finally the day came round unheralded, a day much like any other, when I became aware that I was expected to attend Stranraer Parish Church with Alan, after it had been arranged that our Banns of Marriage would be read on three consecutive Sundays. There was no problem with regard to our being residents of that Parish for the required period of time, and no reason that I could see why our marriage, or rather intended marriage should have any just cause etc., or not fulfil all the necessary requirements. I was well into my twenty-second year and Alan had been twenty-one in the April.

My family accepted my sudden change of heart and likewise did the four Corporals in room 20, but I must confess I was more than a little apprehensive and I certainly had given no thought for the future of either of us. How the news became total knowledge of all and sundry I cannot remember and I feel I can be forgiven that, in view of the hornet's nest which we appeared to have stirred up. Many things were hazy and I cannot recall how I came to have sufficient clothing coupons to buy a white wedding dress and all the trimmings. Rocky looked very upset and glum but made no comment to enlighten me as to why I, a WAAF Corporal, should not marry an Officer — the same rank as he was. After all the other WAAF Corporals had done so, so it wasn't as if I was setting a precedent — and had I not worked hard enough to write my way out of the Station Cookhouse at Tern Hill in about five weeks and gone on to become the youngest WAAF NCO with a top grading?

My WAAF Commanding Officer sent for me first, in fact I seemed to take most of the butt, whilst Alan remained completely unmolested. From the moment I stood opposite her, as she was sitting at her desk, it was very obvious that she had been asked to interview me and that she was ill at ease. She did not waste any time.

"Ah! Corporal Stapley," she began, "I am sure you are aware that we are all more than surprised and somewhat dismayed by the news that you intend to marry Flying Officer Duncan. I understand that you were engaged at the time he came here and you were selected to work on the project with him?"

"That is correct, Ma'am, I was."

"Did something happen to make you change your mind? After all you appeared to be very happy and presumably would have continued to be had you not been given these new duties?" I began to feel slightly roused at being questioned about my personal life and it may well have shown in my response.

"I am very sorry if you disapprove, Ma'am, but actually I am doing what I believe to be the right thing — perhaps there are those who would have preferred me to play around with one man whilst being engaged to another — well, I don't see it that way at all. In fact I decided it would be grossly unfair and certainly out of character for me had I done so."

"Yes," she replied, "I see that looking at the situation from that angle you were probably right in wishing to behave as you have, but don't you think you're rushing your fences? After all you are still very young. To become disengaged is one thing, but to get married is a big step to take. I have sent for you to ask you if you will consider giving the matter more thought and yourself more time?"

"No, Ma'am," I said, "I have given my word now, I cannot keep changing my mind."

We were two unhappy women who, until now, had always held each other in great respect. I was dismissed.

Again, when I related most of this interview to Alan, he did not appear to be the least bit perturbed by it — but suddenly, within hours, he was very obviously distressed. His parents, who had moved from Liverpool to a lovely old farmhouse in Suffolk, were so appalled by his decision to marry me that they intended to catch the first possible train up to Stranraer to discuss the situation with the two of us. Naturally, I was furious. How dare they surmise that because of my background I was not good enough for their eldest son.

Life was so very different all those years ago and to my way of thinking class distinction more obvious. I was still too naive to understand that there were those who, like me, had humble beginnings which they swept under the carpet.

We were to meet his parents in the hotel for dinner, where they intended to stay overnight and leave the next day because their farm could not be left for long, there being no one available to help out during the war. Imagine a young girl setting out under these conditions, to meet her In-Laws-to-be. By now Alan was back to his usual form but try as I might I could not seem to lift myself or stop regarding this meeting as an ordeal. The introductions were made and by now I had been around long enough to know which cutlery to use — in fact they did not show the slightest disappointment in me as being Alan's choice. Yet the questions were not long in coming — all the whys and wherefores, our extreme youth, and when none of these things moved us we were told quite bluntly that they would prefer the marriage not to take place.

The evenings were still light and Al remembered he had some shoes to collect from a cobbler. I think it was along the seafront. Longing to get away, I asked if I might go with him. I just could not get to grips with the situation, nor why his parents had come so far for the sole purpose of breaking us up even before they had even met me. But by now I'd had enough and told Alan so and suggested perhaps we should call it off. I thought of all my previous years and the hard work I had done to come so far. I thought too of the three wonderful men in my past, Mac, whom I had loved most of all. I began to realise now that, had we been left to our own devices I most certainly would have come to the conclusion that we were not suited, not at all right for each other. Alan did not take long to convince me that I should dig my heels in, and because we were receiving so much interference without any plausible reason being given, I did just that. For some reason I wondered if they thought me to be a loose woman, which was stupid when they did not even know me.

When we returned to the hotel, we were both resolute and made it obvious that we were going ahead and I, taking my courage in both hands and surprising even myself, said "I am not pregnant, if that is what you are thinking. In fact I am still a virgin, so you need have no worries on that score. I love my job and I am very happy serving as a WAAF."

The battle was over as far as they were concerned, how could we even guess that maybe it was nothing more than a skirmish? We parted from his parents to cycle back to Castle Kennedy whilst they just stood to bid us farewell, with their parting reminder that if we went ahead then be it on our own heads. The parting was both civil and over formal and the last words they spoke were to wish us happiness and the best of luck. I decided that now we had sealed our fate all would be plain sailing — but oh, dear me, no!

On the next two Sundays we sat well up in the front of the congregation in Stranraer Parish Church and heard our Banns of Marriage called. After the first calling the RAF Commanding Officer sent for me and asked me in the most gentle fashion if I could still not see my way to calling the marriage off. By now I sensed it was something serious. I was all too well aware that RAF Commanding Officers do not concern themselves with such trivia as a WAAF Corporal getting married. If any one of them had given me one good reason as to why we two — Alan and I — should not marry I would have withdrawn, but just to subject us to these constant bouts of criticism only served to make me hopping mad.

For over three years I had given my all, sometimes beyond the call of duty, and worst still was the fact that my third stripe to make me a Sergeant, was well overdue on time basis alone.

How well I recall our coming out of the church into the sunshine after the second reading of our Banns of Marriage.

"Well, just one more Sunday and then we can fix a date," Alan remarked. But once again they proved to be "Famous last words".

Still working on the project together, Monday passed in the usual way. The project was almost concluded, so you can imagine the shock I received when Alan walked into the office on the Tuesday morning and said "The wedding is off, or at least postponed."

For one mad moment I thought he was joking in very bad taste. "But why, Ali? Why?" I asked.

"I've just been told to pack immediately. I've been posted to Northern Ireland." So at last Ireland too was to claim my attention, just as I said it would eventually, in a very unusual way.

"Alan," I asked at last, "is it because you are grounded and are returning to flying again?" I had never broached the subject before.

"I don't know," he said. I had never regarded him as a liar so I wanted to believe him.

"Oh, that's really spiteful, they know the Banns are to be called next Sunday for the third and last time."

Alan made no comment, just seemed to be concentrating on collecting his few belongings in the office. He appeared ill at ease, just as he had been when he first learned that his parents were coming. He was also doing everything with great haste, truly out of character for him. There had been a night only a few weeks earlier, which seemed like an eternity now, when he had chided me by saying, "When I hold you in my arms and kiss you, you just stand there and make me feel it to be a very one-sided affair. You never

J

throw your arms round my neck or take the initiative," and I could not deny the truth of this. But now he looked at me full in the face. "This is not the end, you can be certain of that," he said.

Then it was his turn to give me a perfunctory kiss and with the merest of hugs he went out and quietly closed the door behind him. Another chapter of my life was over.

CHAPTER TWENTY-THREE

UPWARDS AND ONWARDS

My mind went totally blank as if I were in shock and I cannot for the life of me recall who informed me that I was not to be returned to work for Rocky but that I was to be given a real job again as Corporal I/C (in charge) of the Wing Commander's Orderly Room in the next Nissen Hut. Of course, it was still on the engineering side of clerical duties.

First, I went all alone the following Sunday morning and sat, a lonely figure in Stranraer Parish Church, listening to the final calling of our Banns. It was a mere formality now, but once this event was behind me I noticed that there was a change of attitude towards me from all sources. I could sense that the fact was common knowledge, but equally the personnel were as puzzled as I was at this strange turn of events, yet no one mentioned it nor questioned me. I even got the distinct impression that the higher echelons had decided to take some of the blame themselves and were going to great pains to ensure that I was in no way made to feel guilty.

Strangely enough, "Q" did not write to me again at all — yet I wondered why he did not at least pen one letter to try to make me change my mind. He appeared to have accepted his fate as I had mine, with quiet dignity. However, the nine-day wonder soon passed and I was back in full swing, the old me rising like a phoenix from the ashes.

The Wing Commander was a very quiet man who worked alone in his small office. I found I had four members of staff in the long narrow, Orderly Room, which ran the full length, or almost, of the Nissen Hut. My first joy was to discover I had the quickest typist I had ever seen at my service. I will call her Barbara and I know if she recognises herself she will not mind my remarking that she was quite a plain Jane, with straight, mousey-coloured hair, which she dragged back tightly, making her look even more severe. On the one occasion I met her husband, Jim, he too was plain, but theirs was one of those rare marriages made in Heaven, for they doted on each other. How well I remember Barbara's remark, after I had laughingly told her to slow down a bit or there would be sparks coming from her typewriter.

"I just love working for you Corporal, because you never ask any one of us to do something you could not do yourself."

"Well, I couldn't type at that speed for a start!"

"No, perhaps not, but you are so well organised that you never have need to correct us. I notice if something is put back into my "in" tray it has the necessary information to show me that I misunderstood what was wanted. On the other hand, if there are no alterations or comments, I know, without any issue being made of it, that it is not up to the high standards expected."

Yes — there was much more to Barbara's character than one first surmised and this fact was, in time, to be the cause of my becoming VIP once more. But not yet, for I was to remain in that same Orderly Room until late summer.

It was now nearly a year since I had spent that last happy day with Mac and his mother, and by now I realised that I had acted out of character because he had left me in limbo.

One morning when there was a damp chill in the air, Barbara spoke to me very quietly. "Corporal, shouldn't you be having a word with the young WAAF working down at the far end of the office?"

"Why?" I asked. "Has she upset you or some other member of staff in some way?"

To my utter surprise she replied "I don't wish to speak out of order, but I must tell you frankly that, whilst you are the most experienced Corporal with regard to work, in other ways you are very unworldly, otherwise you would know. I would like to add, without meaning to be in the least offensive, that even if you were engaged to F/O Duncan, I could lay it on the line that you are still a virgin."

I burst out laughing and told her that she must start straight away with my first lesson "on the birds and the bees"! But I could not pretend that I did not know what she was telling me.

"Are you going to tell me the exact situation, in strictest confidence, as you know it, or the way you see it?" I asked.

"Well, I was more than a bit alarmed when she started coming in each morning and relating the happenings of the previous night." Here I noticed she blushed profusely before proceeding. "I mean, was it necessary to tell us that he excited her so much it made her toes curl up? I wanted to mention this to you earlier, and now I wish I had for I fear I'm already too late. When she rushes out of the office in the mornings it's because she's suffering from morning sickness."

Barbara was a Leading Aircraftwoman and my second in command, so I asked her to make the suggestion of wanting her lunch hour changed, thus leaving me alone with the young girl in question. I recalled that first November morning on Gas Drill when I had been so naive on this subject, but I did not lack the know-how any more. This was to be the first of two cases I had to deal with — plus one Roll Call thrust on me in an emergency one morning at the house. Each situation was different, of course, and in every case always "too late".

I used the girl's Christian name and asked the simple question "Is there something you would like to talk to me about?" It worked, she just dropped her head onto my shoulder and burst into tears.

"Don't cry," I told her. "It's too late for that, I'll ring Sick Bay whilst we're alone and make an appointment for you to attend." I asked her if she would rather I asked for the Medical Corporal to break the ice by telling her what to expect and she gave me a swift hug.

"Oh! Yes, please," she said through her tears. "That was the part I was dreading."

After that it was out of my hands. Barbara never even questioned me as to what action I had taken and so the matter was closed.

We went along quite normally after that, Barbara taking early lunch each day and aware that she was expected to be in charge whilst I was absent from our small office.

Change was always on the books and often came in unusual circumstances. This is what happened that late summer of 1944. It was believed that the war was hopefully coming to an end and it was decided to dispense with personnel who worked on some of the administration duties. Only the very best essential staff remained, but no one could yet be dismissed from the service. This meant that many of varying rank and duties had to be found other employment. As normal in such cases, one tends to shrug one's shoulders and not to fully comprehend the situation. However, the change was to affect me immediately as a Sergeant WAAF was allocated to our section and I found myself serving with someone senior in rank but officially U/T (Under Training) as a Clerk/General Duties. As I have already said, I was always inclined to be subservient to both senior ranks and situations, so I was prepared to soldier on in this unusual situation.

It worked for only a few weeks, with the Sergeant taking the noon till one o'clock lunch, as did Barbara, whilst I went for the one till two o'clock as before, when the Sergeant returned. It was during my absence that Barbara got into a blazing row with the Sergeant. The Wing Commander heard every word as he passed the open office door to reach his own small office.

When I returned, completely oblivious as to what Barbara had said, I barely had time to sense the atmosphere before the Wing Commander's bell rang. I suppose, with the best will in the world, I was finding it hard not to get the odd "dig" in, so I simply said, "The bell, Sergeant." The Sergeant returned almost immediately and told me that the Wing Commander wanted me. He was a short, rotund man, quiet, and a gentleman with a capital "G".

"Have you been told what happened during your absence at lunch?" he asked, and I shook my head in bewilderment. "I can well imagine why your staff are loyal to you, but Barbara laid herself wide open for being put on a charge by the Sergeant, 'though I don't dispute that what she said in anger is true. Apparently, the poor Sergeant was already feeling out of her depth, so she did not need to be reminded by an LACW that she was getting a Sergeant's pay whilst a Corporal was doing most of the work. As if that was not bad enough, she had also been informed 'We were all happy here before you came to take over!' " The Wing Commander spoke with the wisdom of Solomon. "I think it would be better if you came in here to work with me," he said. "I have had a plan in mind for quite some time that I would like to put into operation."

My heart sank — I had only been free such a short while since my work with Alan on the Project and now I would be working on my own once more.

I never returned to the Engineering Orderly Room. In next to no time a board was mounted on a wall in the Wing Commander's Office and on it I was to chart the history of each individual aircraft and its whereabouts at any given time with a display of multicoloured pins. Each colour denoted an engine change, aircraft frame or engine repair, ailerons; whether the craft was fit for flying, which hangar it was housed in — all could be seen at a glance. The dreaded black pins denoted a prang. The job was easy enough, though I did stand in some awe lest I made a mistake. It also became tedious because it left me with far too much spare time to while away. Added to this, I noticed the Wing Commander was absent more and more from his office and knowing him to be a rather shy person I naturally assumed that the move was not to his liking and that he much preferred working on his own. I never went into the Orderly Room, though I was frequently asked questions connected with the day-to-day running of it. But in the life we lived there was constant change and mine came yet again when I least expected it to.

The Wing Commander came into the office one day and asked me if I intended going to see "The Mikado", which was the latest camp concert already billed up on posters. I said, truthfully, that I knew very little about the theatre, and then surprisingly he gave me two complementary tickets saying doubtless I could find someone to attend with me. I asked Barbara, I felt I owed her that, at least.

When we arrived the next night, we were impressed and flattered to find that we had been allocated two of the best seats in the Hall. Later someone came and brought us each a free programme. The curtain rose on "The Mikado" and it was not very long before the two of us were gasping with surprise when Nanki-poo arrived on the scene — a short, rotund Nanki-poo, complete with plaited pigtail hanging down his back and singing with such a beautiful voice.

"Oh! Barbara, isn't the Wing Commander marvellous? Such a wizard voice — he has certainly been taking us for a ride!" Until that night I had only ever seen "The Quaker Girl" as a thirteen-year-old member of the Girls' Friendly Society, and at that age I had been romantically enchanted with its song "Will you not come to the ball", but I knew that after seeing "The Mikado" I would remain hooked on both music and the theatre for the rest of my life, and this has been so.

It was obvious that the Wing Commander was highly amused by his small deception and was even more so when I confessed that, due to his frequent absenteeism, when he was away at practice, I had begun to have doubts about my having BO. He really chuckled at that!

It was a short time after that night that that he arrived at the office one morning and promptly said "Be honest, now Corporal, you are bored out of your mind working on my chart. I had a few words over breakfast with the CO about you and, like me, he sympathises with you with regard to the outcome of recent events. We are both well aware that your third stripe is well overdue on time basis alone, but the longer the war goes on the fewer the vacancies which become available. However, he did telephone Group HQ and asked if they could find you a position more suited to your talents and training and I was told to ask you if you would like to return to your own country?'' This was the longest speech I had ever heard the Wing Commander make. I knew my heart was still locked in that small office, (no place on the camp would be such a shrine, as once again I relived that startling day almost a year ago when I had picked up my telephone to hear the voice of my Mac come through to me as I looked out on my brambles and he was full of such high spirits and asked me to go to him.)

"Where would I go, anyway, to find such a position?'' The offer, when finalised, was one I could not refuse. I was to return to Gloucestershire, close to where it had all begun in April, 1941, but this time I would stay overnight. The next day I would be posted out to one of the Satellite Dromes, where I would be in charge of my own small Orderly Room. I was to learn later that to make this position possible for me a male Corporal had been posted overseas, a real compliment since it was now late in the summer of 1944. I knew I would miss the other four Corporals in room 20, Dunragit House, most of all, as they watched me pack my full kit for the last time in Scotland at the end of nearly a year's service there. I said a special "Goodbye'' and offered my sincere thanks to one of the nicest Officers for whom I had worked. In return he wished me better luck, then I left for the HQ Orderly Room for my documentation and arranged to have my cycle sent on later by another train.

I was leaving behind me my broken engagement to "Q'' and my Banns of Marriage called in Stranraer Parish Church, but most of all my heart — and the poignant memory of a last kiss on Ayr Railway Station. Alan was still in Ireland and yet I must admit I was leaving with a sense of peace and relief prevailing and the pleasing knowledge that I would soon be taking over from a male Corporal so would have to be on my mettle. I mentally rolled up my sleeves!

CHAPTER TWENTY-FOUR

INTERMISSION

I arrived at Little Rissington late in the day and knew I must sleep overnight until transport became available to take me to "Windrush" next morning. Here, I must confess, just as I never really got to know Wales and Anglesey well, neither did I learn until years long after the war had ended, there is a pretty, small village tucked away, and a river, both known as Windrush.

To say I was appalled by the hut bearing the legend "Orderly Room" would be an understatement — I was horrified. I had never seen any place so unworthy of its name. I got on the blower and informed my superiors that there was no way I could possibly do any office work there until we were sent our full office supplies. I listed the latter, and then gave a verbal description of what passed as a typewriter, not least that it was a ton weight. We were all pleasantly surprised when the truck arrived next morning and all our needs were aboard, right down to a decent typewriter. We stripped the cupboards and filing cabinets bare and then worked well into the evening stocking them again with our brand-new supplies. When we finally cut the first stencil for our first Personnel Occurrence Report it was like giving birth to a baby as we proudly despatched it and extra copies via the truck to all those concerned.

I was walking one evening over the wet grass when I heard someone call my name and found it to be the WAAF Commanding Officer in a very friendly mood. "How are you liking it here, Corporal?" she asked and she laughed when I replied "Oh! I love the job, it's what I was trained to do and the one I love best of all. Just think, I'm only a WAAF Corporal, yet I have my very own little Orderly Room."

"Is that where you are off to now?" she asked and I grinned.

"I nearly sleep there. I hate the place, I feel I have been dumped down in some big, lush green field and perpetually walking through wet grass." But little did I guess that I would not remain there very long as once more I became VIP. Yes, my war was one all of its own, nobody had one quite like mine. My documents must show exactly how long I stayed at Windrush, a mere three or four weeks at most.

I picked up the telephone one morning to be asked by the Sergeant at Rissy "Are you going to keep this up?" Puzzled, I asked him what he meant.

"We have never once received a POR from Windrush," he went on to say, "and now they are arriving with amazing regularity."

"Well, isn't that what I was trained for?" I asked. "I, who started my service working in a Cookhouse, now have my very own little Orderly Room, of which I am justly proud."

"Well, I have news for you — the Commanding Officer and I are impressed and have decided you could manage the larger Orderly Room and personnel on the Chipping Norton Satellite Drome." I heard him give a slight chuckle. "It would mean posting yet another male Corporal overseas again."

"You're joking, aren't you?" I asked.

"Would I joke about a thing like that?" he said, still chuckling.

I jumped in quickly and said "Oh, yes please."

"Then post yourself back on tomorrow's POR and come back with it on tomorrow's truck. You'll need to sleep here overnight, I'll arrange that, and leave for 'Chippy' the next day."

I could hardly sleep for excitement. Never mind about the lack of my third stripe — they had kept their promise to me with regard to my having an appointment to satisfy me, and now I was to have another, bigger Orderly Room.

Even something as simple as my exchanging Satellites was not without incident. The next morning I was strolling round the camp when I fell to wondering why an LACW was doing likewise. She was reading a billboard so I stopped to ask her if she could not find a better way to spend her day off.

"Oh, hello Corporal," she said. "Actually, I am not on day off, I'm just filling in time until I leave tomorrow to go to the Satellite Drome at Chipping Norton."

"What trade are you?" I asked, and she told me she was a Clerk/General Duties.

"You wouldn't be going there to work in the Orderly Room by any chance, because if you are, then meet your new boss." Still studying the poster she asked me if I happened to know the words of the song from the advertised camp show and I laughingly told her that I couldn't sing a note myself but had a good ear when listening to others singing — and I do have another talent, I can remember lyrics.

"Oh, please tell me that you know the words of one of my favourite Richard Tauber songs, 'We are in Love With You, My Heart and I'."

"Yes, I can recall all of the words of that song," I said, so we spent the next half hour finding paper and committing them to it.

Thus I came to meet Rosa, who quickly confided in me that her names were Rose Amy on her documents, but as she disliked both of them she had taken the "e" off Rose and added the "a" off Amy, so Rosa was born.

We travelled out together the next day and though we did not know it then we were to become firm friends and remain together until we were demobilised. Rosa was my typist. I also had another WAAF, who was of lower rank but held down a very responsible job. She remained with her desk permanently in the Adjutant's Office, as all her work was highly confidential — covering Discharges, especially from pregnancies, Serious Charges and Courts Martial but they, luckily were very rare.

We went straight into the same ritual I had requested when stocking up at Windrush and again we set to in our bigger OR as soon as the stock arrived by truck. At last I felt I had found my forte and no longer bellyached over my long overdue third stripe to make me up to a Sergeant. Besides Rosa, I had a wonderful cheery Cockney, with red hair and freckles, but unlike Ricky at Tern Hill, this one was more than just a runner to do the messages and odd jobs. He was a very friendly, capable man and he worked mainly on "Leave Passes". Try as I might I could never understand why his desk, immediately behind my own, faced the wall, nor could I get him to change it.

I must make it quite clear from the outset that no one, not even the Officers, had any knowledge of the events which preceded my posting from RAF Castle Kennedy. It was accepted that I was a WAAF Corporal, with a Grade "A" pass and they therefore worked for me under the illusion that this was my sole purpose for being there and why two male Corporals had been posted overseas this late in the war. In fact, they seemed more duly proud of the fact than I was.

There was another person with whom we all came into contact most mornings and evenings — he was an Italian POW. As far as I was concerned it was hopeless from the start, for me he was just another young Italian fighting for his country, as I was for mine. He was young, with a kindly personality and showed no animosity but loved every minute he could hang around the Orderly Room. He cleaned the office in wintertime and made us the most extravagant fires, which all but scorched our legs. We soon found him an enorous enamel mug and after tea was made, somewhat early since we had all enjoyed a decent breakfast, his mug was filled to the brim, and though he barely understood any English, his eyes were so full of gratitude that I found my own eyes filled with tears. Twice I was rebuked by the Adjutant on this subject, and rightly so, of course. He made it quite clear to our POW that he must leave the OR at once — but when I got caught unashamedly the second time, the Adjutant appeared to accept the situation and overlooked it.

I had a photo of Ali in a wooden frame on my desk, without the protection of glass and it soon became furled by the intense heat from the fires. To my utter astonishment I turned in for work one morning to find that, after our POW had finished cleaning the OR the night before, he had taken the photo in its frame. He had found some small lengths of multicoloured wools and must have sat well into the night and woven them across each corner of the frame. They even had some semblance of a pattern with regards to his use of colours. Where he had managed to get this wool from was to remain a mystery, but his delight when he witnessed my astonishment, was something to behold. The photograph remained like that for many, many years after the war ended, but eventually fell prey to the moths in the attic of an old house in which we had lived. Yet I never saw it without remembering the POW struggling with English sufficient enough to say "You like, Kapperal?" Sometimes I would ponder about him, what was his name and did he return safely to his native Italy?

Rosa was as near to being a blonde as I, with my darkish hair, was to being a brunette. It was obvious early on that men found her very attractive, not least the Officers. Her facial bone structure was unusual and her nose, almost aquiline, added to her charming attraction, though no one would have described her as being pretty. Remembering our first meeting I was not surprised to find that she had more than a passing interest in anything theatrical. How it came to pass that we both managed to get the same day off I cannot recall, but we did and she invited me to go along with her to one of the nearby Cotswold towns, to collect her tap shoes, which she had taken to be repaired.

I was always happy in her company and was thoroughly enjoying being with her away from the atmosphere of the office. After she had collected her shoes I asked her what she had in mind to do next. She surprised me by saying she would pop into a Chemist shop to see if there was any stage make-up available. I nearly laughed in her face, for even by Rosa's standards it sounded more zany than usual.

The lady assistant was neither young nor small, but she had a beaming countenance and lovely thick Cotswold accent. I listened as Rosa made her request and got the expected negative reply by being informed (as if we did not know it already) that stage make-up was scarce and only sold to those in the legitimate theatre.

What followed made that day very memorable, as Rosa asked me to stand up. She promptly sat down on the chair I had just vacated and donned her newly-repaired tap shoes.

"Well, I am legitimate theatre," she said. "Watch this!" The shopkeeper was as astonished as I was when, in that tiny space, Rosa went into her tap dancing routine. Both fascinated, the woman took time out to call her husband. "Dad, come and look at this!"

He came and we left with some stage make-up!

There was another memorable occasion connected with Rosa. She had travelled the twenty miles or so into Oxford alone on her day off and came back looking a million dollars, having had her hair attended to by hairdressers with obvious experience. It was run by two French brothers, Pierre and Andre. Her hair did look really lovely, but I was more interested in her story about the brother who had obviously been charmed by her too and tried to date her. With no thought of *"Amour"* in mind I decided I would go and have my hair done there when I next went to Oxford. It was probably partly out of sheer curiosity and partly sheer vanity, for how many times had I been told that my hair was beautiful when I dropped it from its retaining ribbon and it fell in long natural curls and waves? I was to remember that trip, nevertheless, because it was so long since I had been to other than the camp hairdresser. I normally looked after it myself. I completely forgot that, once under the drier, although I appeared not to be shouting, I was. I had the whole clientele by their ears as they listened to my version of Rosa and the two French brothers. No wonder everyone looked so delighted and amused, especially when I was shown to the door and given a deep bow, with a request to come again soon.

Rosa's life story up till then as I remember it, was that she was born in the East End of London, where as a child she had danced for pennies in the street. Later her family moved to Nottingham where her father, who had only one arm, packed parcels with meticulous care. I found this hard to swallow until, one such parcel arrived for her, the like of which I had never seen before, nor ever since. Her typing was not up to the extremely high standard set by Barbara, but then they were in no way alike at all.

Our Commanding Officer had his office at the far end of the Nissen Hut, the Adjutant and the "Confidential Clerk" were first on the left, whilst opposite them was the Assistant Adjutant's Office on the right side, as was the Orderly Room, a hatch connecting the offices. The Assistant Adjutant was really dishy, both to look at and to work for. Our WAAF Commanding Officer was nearly opposite the Orderly Room, then there was a break for the Entrance/Exit, beyond which was another LACW, who worked alone as my Documents' Clerk. Then came the Station W/Officer and finally the telephone exchange — we were a compact little bunch. It was here that I reached the conclusion that to be just a Corporal with one's own little Orderly Room was to live an idyllic working life.

I recall the Adjutant once saying to me "Whenever tea or coffee is requested it arrives with amazing regularity and complete with both milk and sugar — I feel there must be a fiddle going on somewhere but I dare not ask in case you dry up on me!" It was the accepted thing, we held the Aces — all "five" of them, so we could cut through red tape as if it were mere bagatelle. If a member of the kitchen staff arrived to collect their Leave Pass early, we were always asked what we were short of. Even I was amazed by the number of personnel who claimed to have lengthy journeys to Scotland.

The Police were just as accommodating. "You send down our passes and we'll see who needs to get away early."

But we drew the line at outright dishonesty. One such case was when I had done the Leave Passes myself, booked them in in the Orderly Room and sent them down to the Guardroom, where they were booked in and out again.

Thus there came this day when our system proved foolproof, when an Aircrew Flight Sergeant altered my 7th to the 9th, unaware that when he returned to try and bluff his way out of why he had taken two extra days and was therefore AWOL, he found that the Police Records matched mine. He was soon put on a Charge. It was rare for the Commanding Officer to officiate on such an occasion but this time he did, and I was called as a witness and asked to draw my normal figure seven on the blackboard behind the Commanding Officer. This was compared to the one which had very obviously been altered into a nine.

We wanted for nothing and indeed another bounty fell into our laps when we were allocated twenty tickets, free of charge, so that we could visit the theatre in Oxford to see well-known actors and actresses. We enjoyed seeing John Geilgud (not then Sir), Flora Robson, (not then a Dame) and many others. We did have one great disappointment and that was when we went to see the very beautiful actress, Vivien Leigh, in "The Skin of Our Teeth". It was not only our party and some from RAF Kiddlington who were bored through lack of understanding the plot — we began to notice large numbers of the public leaving the theatre. Being in charge, I was being bombarded on all sides for permission to do likewise. At first I thought in terms of decorum, after all the tickets were free, but I soon became aware that there were those who were willing to leave with, or without, my permission, so sadly we all trooped out a bit shamefaced. Even after the war had ended I made time to try to get to grips with it and sort it out, but I did not manage to do so and to this day remain totally ignorant of what it was all about.

If I had been asked to choose whom I most enjoyed and who left me with a lasting memory it would, without a doubt, have been Flora Robson. She appeared to me to be a truly wonderful actress, plain maybe, but so excellent at her craft.

CHAPTER TWENTY-FIVE

FIRE DRILL

My personal life appeared to have come full circle, for as soon as Olive was aware that I was stationed in Oxfordshire, she invited me to meet her for luncheon and in no time she asked me to stay at "Orchard Cottage" on an extended weekend. Our talk was mostly of Stanley and happier days there. Olive had taken a job in the Fur Department of a large store, long since disappeared, to help her alleviate her great sorrow over the loss of her much-loved only son, only twenty-one years old when he was killed. I could not see any lessening of her sorrow, but merely working as a furrier helped to fill her days. She had only one hour for lunch so if I went down by bus to see her it was best for us to meet up at "The Cadena" for lunch, another sadly missed meeting place, which was later to disappear too. It must have been about this time that I mentioned in passing my favourite song at that moment was "Fascination". I thought nothing of my remark, little dreaming that it was to make me VIP as in the old days. With so little time we would meet up at The Cadena and I thought nothing of it when the doorman requested my name and whether I was meeting Mrs Colbert inside. I agreed that all this was correct but was totally unprepared when he led me inside, a mere WAAF Corporal and told me our table was right down near the three/four-piece music ensemble. I blushed to the roots of my hair as I removed my cap and realised a piece of red carpet had been hurriedly laid down within. The nod was given as I went forward to join Olive and I saw her away ahead of me, beaming at her ruse, as the music was suddenly switched to "Fascination". It was the nearest I had ever come to being a celebrity! So much for fame.

Olive preferred me to go to the Cottage and she was very curious about this Officer to whom I had so unexpectedly become engaged and bade me take him there if an opportunity presented itself. I, on the other hand, was very happy the way things were, and scarcely thought about anything but work.

I still loved Mondays, when we were automatically confined to Billets for the evening, for the same reasons as before, cleaning our bed spaces and doing our domestic chores, including washing and ironing. The pressing of our suits was done in another hut and it was here that I received such a strong electric shock from a faulty iron that I thought I was a goner. How different from the early days in married quarters at Tern Hill, when against all the rules all sorts of electrical gadgets were hidden deep inside every possible hiding place — especially electric irons.

I had made it a rule that no WAAF who worked with me would be accepted as a member of the hut of which I was in charge. This was for several reasons, mainly that on a Satellite Drome, although only a Corporal, I was as good as the "Queen Bee". We held documentation of all members of other ranks and these documents were at my disposal, which led to the second rule: If any WAAF ever came to me and questioned me on the matter of another WAAF, I would not tolerate any such approach being made. I pointed out that it was in their own interests, for if I was fair to one, then obviously I would treat each of them with the same confidence. They saw and accepted my reasoning, so that I never once had the slightest trouble. Yet they knew some horseplay and the odd bit of leg-pulling fell in line, so it was, all in all, a very happy existence.

Strangely enough, although willing to do my own bed space, as I always did in the past, I was never allowed to do so. All Corporals had the same arrangement, where their beds ran lengthways down the hut, creating an unusual small alcove for personal belongings. Here we were blessed — or so I thought at the time — with a good length of shelf fitted on the wall over our beds, made of a wide piece of wood. I kept my gas mask, tin helmet and gym shoes on mine. The young WAAF who was in the first bed on the same side as my own always said each Monday "Don't worry about your bed space, Corporal, after I've done mine I'll organise someone to help me with yours." She added "You just sit there on your bed and talk to us, I just love listening to you." She was a Geordie and so had the mistaken idea that I was, to use her word, "posh". I did not realise just how ingrained this idea was, that anyone who came from Southern England was "posh" until one night she said to me "What was that you said, Corporal?" Puzzled, I told her that I was not aware that I had said anything extraordinary. "But you mentioned your sister and you haven't got any brothers or sisters,"

K

she said, to my surprise. "You're an only child, aren't you?"

"Good gracious, no," I replied. "You name them and I've got them! Two sisters left, plus two half-sisters, as well as both stepbrothers and stepsisters too."

She sat on her bed looking at me in disbelief. "Well, that really is incredible," she commented after a while. "You always have the air of being an only child who has been well educated."

"Thank you," I said. "I hope you are not too disillusioned."

Always short of money, she was to remain an ACH/GD, Grade 5, for her full service life. She was no cadger, indeed I would go as far as to say she never shirked anything, but there were times, mostly on those Monday nights, but sometimes on other occasions, when she would ask "Have you got a cigarette, or one you could cut in half and share with me?" and she even resorted to using up my "dub-ends". However, none of this had any other connotation than mutual feelings of respect and affection for each other.

It was one of those Monday nights when I decided to stand on my bed to reach up and clean the shelf above it. My bed was near the door and so was the Hut Fire-extinguisher, so I was shattered when my tin helmet slipped out of my hands. We had been taught little couplets to help us to memorise the usuage of the different types of extinguishers, and most popular and best remembered was "If it is red, bang it on its head". Well, I certainly had no reason to recall that couplet for I watched with horror as my helmet, seemingly well versed in the Drill, landed in such a way that the hard rim hit the extinguisher and scored a bull's-eye.

Talk about panic — the foam gushed out in all directions as I lifted it and swung it round to get it through the door, which a quick-witted WAAF had opened, but not before splashing walls, ceiling and floor.

Next morning our WAAF Commanding Officer accepted the accident with good humour. She told me to ring the Fire Section and get a member of their staff to call and collect a chit from her authorising them permission to enter WAAF quarters.

All would have been well but for the fact that in a very short space of time I did a repeat performance. This time we were much quicker springing into action but once outside the hut the extinguisher persisted to gush until it was empty once more. Even I, the Queen Bee of the Orderly Room, dared not chance my luck a second time, so I rang the Fire Section myself.

"This is the Orderly Room Corporal," I said.

"Had any more accidents lately with your extinguisher?" asked their sectional Corporal, before I could utter another word.

"Well, yes I have and that's why I'm phoning you. I did it again last night, and I haven't the guts to tell our CO again." After a little laughing session he said, "Leave it with me, I've got an idea, but don't let on you know! I will ring her myself and say that when we were recently on the WAAF site the thought had arisen that it was some time since we had checked all the extinguishers. Then I'll ask for permission to inspect each hut for the sake of safety."

Once again it worked like a charm, he just switched mine and reported all was well. When he telephoned me the "all clear" he added "That's one you owe me, Corporal" and that's proof of how the system worked.

As far as we were concerned, the incident was closed — but it wasn't, as I was to find out many weeks later.

CHAPTER TWENTY-SIX

SCARLET AND GREEN

My Documents' Clerk was always a little abrasive toward me and Rosa told me that it was because she held my own documents and felt that I had become a Corporal from starting off as an ACH/GD in a Cookhouse, whilst she still remained an LACW for far too long. The fact that my third stripe was overdue seemed in no way to pacify her feelings, but I gather my staff "had a gentle go at her", telling her that I was in no way to blame for these circumstances. After that she settled down, and though never bosom pals, we were able to get along reasonably well. I rang her one day, although her office was only three or four offices down the passage — we never walked anywhere if we could use a telephone — and she was both surprised and interested when I asked her to look up the documents of a certain L/Aircraftman and told her in which section he worked.

"Have you got a date with him, Corporal?" she asked. "I didn't think dating was your scene."

"Well, let's just say he thinks he has a date with the Orderly Room Corporal on the promise that he assures me he can get me into his section, which we all know is forbidden territory." She read out all the pertinent points about him.

"Please let me know how it goes," she went on to say.

He took me to the cinema in Chipping Norton, but it was not long before he became what we all termed a "me, me, me, man" as we walked back to camp. If I hadn't been up to a slight piece of mischief by intending to put a dent in his pride, I would have been bored out of my mind. To top it all he commenced on a long diatribe about his interest in amateur dramatics, and when we reached the road leading up to HQ — not the WAAF Quarters, he meant this to imply that he really was going to take me where he had promised.

148

Firstly, he suggested we stand beside a small wooden paling which was a bit sheltered as it had a tree hanging over it. Even I was not prepared for what happened next. He suddenly burst into song. I just stood there struck dumb although, to be fair, his voice was passable. We then got onto the subject of books and I confessed that I had never mastered completely the reading of *"Gone With The Wind"*.

"Oh, isn't that lucky?" he said, "I keep my copy in my section. Shall I send it to the Orderly Room tomorrow?"

"Oh, couldn't I pick it up when you show me round your section?" I said, with all innocence.

"No, no," he said, "I'll send it down first thing in the morning." So I still hadn't pricked his balloon, but I knew I had one ace to play. I told you that we in the Orderly Room held all the Aces, all "five" of them. Sure enough I found myself closed in when he put a hand either side of me on the fence and leaned forwards to kiss me.

"Ah hah!" I said "I don't think your wife would approve of that!"

"But I'm not married, Corporal," he replied, much as I had expected.

"Oh, dear, I'll have to get the alteration made on your documents in the morning," I responded.

"You win, I forgot you have access to total knowledge about me."

He was hurt, well, I suspect it was just his pride. For all that he was a bighead he took my rebuke well and though I never got into his section, nor ever expected I would, he did keep his promise and his copy of *"Gone With The Wind"* arrived next day in the Orderly Room. I kept it in my desk drawer, not that I would find as much time to read it as I had long ago when I read *"One Passionate Year"* in Central Registry as a very "rookie" WAAF way back in the spring of 1941 at RAF Tern Hill.

However, I was skimming through the pages one day and had not noticed that the hatch to the Assistant Adjutant's Office was open, so I little guessed I was being overheard when I made my announcement to the staff.

"When this blasted war is over I want to live like Scarlett O'Hara. Just imagine me in a beautiful crinoline gown making my entrance down a magnificent flight of stairs." When the bell rang I went into the Assistant Adjutant's Office.

"Oh! Please do come in, Miss Scarlett," he greeted me. "I'm so sorry but I happen to have some urgent work that needs your attention." He was very young, very tall and very handsome and as time went by he proved to be the least stuffy of all.

As my Documents' Clerk had remarked, dating was a rare event for me at this time. My life revolved round the Orderly Room during the day and in my hut with my girls each night. I did, however, make various sorties into the surrounding counties and twice when on Crewe Station I was to become VIP as of old.

The first occasion was when I was travelling on a very crowded train and found myself squeezed tightly in the corridor against a young woman wearing civvies. It was rare for anyone not in uniform to start up a conversation with those of us who were, but this was the exception to the rule. Normally good tempered, I must have found this journey more tedious than usual.

"Never mind how far I have yet to travel," I said to her, "I've two blasted hours to wait on Crewe Station and you know what a hellhole that is."

"Oh, I am sorry, I live close to the station and I'd love to take you home for tea and to meet my mother." I felt really humbled and dreadful and started explaining that I could not accept her unexpected invitation as there would be all sorts of problems involved, not least getting out and then back in again through the ticket barrier.

"That's the least of your worries," she remarked. "Come on, you'll see."

When we reached the ticket collector I was taken aback.

"Hello, Dad," she said to him. "I'm just taking this young WAAF home for tea, see you later!"

I remember it was still light enough for me to see the row of terraced houses and notice that her home was the smartest in the row. She let us into the hall.

"Hello, Mum," she called out. "I've brought a visitor for tea."

I was totally bewildered by it all. Her mother was beaming as she greeted me and asked my name and if I would like to pop upstairs to freshen up. In all I made two trips upstairs and because this was late summer, 1944, I remember how impressed I was by the fact that I was seeing a coloured bathroom suite for the first time in my life. It impressed me so much that when I wrote my doggerel because I was moved by the experience I ended it by rhyming the word Crewe with "the fact that I remembered most was the colour of their loo!" Whether this came under my happiness, sadness or just plain comic doggerel I don't know, though I would think the latter. The bathroom suite was green!

They asked me if I would prefer to have them use my Christian name, more friendly they thought than just Corporal, but I did feel terribly guilty when I arrived in the dining room to find one of their precious eggs had been boiled for me. When I demurred I was told not to worry as they kept a few hens out the back. Whilst we were eating there came the sound of "Dad" letting himself in, obviously one of the members of staff on Crewe Station and later, by which time it was getting a little dark, he walked with me back to the station and made sure I had no problem with my ticket.

The second incident I can recall very vividly. It was a dull, cold dreary Sunday and everything was shut right down, even the waiting rooms. Again I had a long wait but what was worse was that it was almost eerie to find this normally busy junction as bare and quiet as a morgue. I sat down on a seat feeling really sorry for myself, but soon the bitter wind made me think I might find it a little more sheltered if I moved to the seat on the other side of the waiting room. To my amazement I found I was not alone after all. An RAF Officer sat huddled so deeply into his greatcoat that only his cap gave me any indication of his rank. Sensing movement, he lifted his head just sufficiently to see if anyone really was there and then, without warning he startled me by saying "Well, I'll be blowed, if it isn't dear old 'Luscious'!" We sat for a while discussing why and for how long we were likely to be on Crewe Station.

"Come on, Luscious," he said. "Let's forget about this drafty place and find a hotel in the town where they might rustle us up some lunch," adding thoughtfully, "my treat, of course." So, though I never saw either of my Squadron Leaders again, here was my Flight Lieutenant, whose handwriting had tripped me up on my first day as an NCO, sharing a delicious roast beef luncheon with me, and what is more, delighted to have me for company. It was a really lovely occasion, but I never saw him again after that Sunday on Crewe Station.

CHAPTER TWENTY-SEVEN

THE UNEXPECTED

Likewise, coincidences occurred in the Orderly Room. One of these came about because all other ranks, up to and including Corporal used the last three figures of their service number. Now well into my fourth year I had never once seen my 964 on any other of the vast number of documents I had handled. Here, at last, was just such a person, but what amused me more was the fact that its owner was aptly named Sergeant Quirk. Of course, he had no way of knowing any of this when he reported to the Orderly Room and I greeted him.

"Ah! Yes, Sergeant Quirk, 964, I believe?"

"Good God," he said, "I've heard about your phenomenal retentive memory — can you do that to every member of staff on the camp?"

"No, you are very special," I told him. "You are the first member of staff I have ever come across in all the years I've handled documents who shares my last three figures of 964. I thought it a very apt and quirky coincidence and quite extraordinary."

It was a fact that all too often it was said, "Ask Corporal, she'll know," and hence I was often put upon. However, one morning I arrived about an hour late, just as I had warned my staff that I would, as I had a dental appointment. As I was walking back to HQ, I was recalling another dental appointment I had attended when I was in Shropshire and how I had returned to my office in tears. When my Squadron Leader noticed my distress and asked me the reason for it, I told him that I had refused the treatment offered as I had been told that I was to have black fillings in my front teeth. When I had protested I had been told that RAF dentists did not do cosmetic dentistry. My Squadron Leader soon bawled the dentist out — so loudly as to make the telephone almost superfluous —

and I was sent back to get my white fillings. Nothing quite so dramatic had happened to upset me this time, so I was feeling quite happy until I opened the Orderly Room door.

"And what the Hell do you call this?" I asked, as I looked aghast at the total disorder. "That isn't a legend on the door, it means what it says, 'Orderly Room' and you are all well aware of that."

"But, Corporal," they all chorused, "someone is on a charge and we've been sorting out the documents."

"So, who's on a charge, then?" I enquired. We had three "Smiths" on the Satellite and, of course, it just had to be one of them. "And whose documents have you sent in?" I asked. To my horror they named the section and I nearly went berserk.

"In Heaven's name, you should have known that it wouldn't be that Smith." I quickly walked along to the Adjutant's Office, gave a peremptory knock and passed the male Sergeant who was preferring the charge and discussing it with the Adjutant. I leaned over his desk. "Wrong documents, Sir," I said and picked them up and put the right ones in place.

The look on the Sergeant's face seemed to express that I might be the next one on the "fizzer", but the Adjutant saved the day. "If Corporal says they are, then they are, for she's like a bloody walking encyclopedia. She even knows where the Smiths are."

With that I closed the door and left to get my Orderly Room shipshape and Bristol fashion again.

But I was not infallible. There was a day when the Adjutant burst into our office nearly apoplectic and threw some paper on my desk. "Who is responsible for this utter rubbish?" he enquired, hyperbole being one of his traits.

It was handwritten so it was obvious to him that the fault or error, was mine, so just as I was about to admit it and apologise, to the amazement of us all my clerk-cum-runner jumped up behind me. "Sorry, Sir, the mistake is mine," he said, following the old rule of protecting someone wearing chevrons. But what utter madness to do so when the someone was me, with my own very distinctive handwriting.

It appeared to wind the Adjutant too, for as he opened the door to leave, he called back "I'll say this for you, Corporal, you certainly have a loyal staff."

"What the Hell made you make such a mad, if gallant gesture?" I asked "H".

"Well, I figure it this way, Corporal, I have no stripes to lose but I do have some pubs in the East End, if they're still standing. Who knows, I might have got more than just 'Jankers' — I might even have got dismissed from the service in time, and I do miss that kind of life." Of course, in the event, nothing further was said.

The summer weather was fading fast, when to our dismay we learned that our WAAF CO had decided that we should get into our gym kit as she felt we could all do with some organised exercise. There was only a minute concrete patch on WAAF Quarters, but it was here we were told to report before going to breakfast in the Cookhouse on the main site. What a nightmare it became for me. Never very sporty, this was not my kind of scene at all. One of the Sergeants began giving us various orders and all went well until she asked us to jump up and down. Several of us were horrified as we found that as we complied so our gym shoes disintegrated and fell apart. The incidents with the fire-extinguisher were to blame, the acid in the foam had been slowly rotting our unused gym shoes away during the past weeks. Luckily for me, our Commanding Officer, believing there was only the one incident which I had reported, wrote them off as an accident, but it really was a funny sight and we could barely refrain from giggling!

My Clerk/Typist approached me one morning and asked if she might have a private word with me.

"Fire ahead," I said. "What's on your mind?"

"Well, I now see the real sense of your not allowing those who work with you to share your hut, but I have three choices. It concerns the WAAF who sleeps in the next bed to mine in my hut. I have been worrying about her for quite some time because she is arriving back later and later, even for a shiftworker. It used to be about 2 a.m. but now it is often 4 a.m. At first I thought I'd mention it to the Corporal in charge of our hut, then I thought maybe it should be her sectional Corporal, but in the end I felt I only wanted to ask your opinion and maybe for your help." She added those same fatal words I had heard before, "I think I might well be too late already."

"The only course open to me is to tell her sectional Corporal," I said. "She is a close buddy of mine, as you well know, and she'll handle the affair and leave us both out of the situation."

"Oh, thank you," she said, "I feel happier doing it this way."

"From now on you must not mention what has been spoken this morning to anyone," I added. "I do trust you, but I have no option but to warn you."

She said she understood that I was speaking to her as an NCO and not as the familiar Corporal for whom she worked.

We all three knew it was an Officer and who he was, but when the WAAF went up before our WAAF Commanding Officer, nothing would make her divulge the name of her lover as he was married and not even British.

So, weeks passed with plenty happening but nothing of any great moment. I was still meeting Olive as often as I could in Oxford and she persuaded me to indulge in a short fur coat from her departmental store, so I looked really swish on my days off. But nothing lasts forever and when the change came it was as unexpected as it was startling.

I picked up my telephone one day thinking it would be just another routine call. I could hardly believe what I was hearing — it was Alan on the line. I should have been excited, just as I had been on that far-off day when my Mac had taken me by surprise in my little office with my brambles on the clay bank outside of the small window. I was surrounded by my staff.

"Where are you?" I asked and he told me he was in Scotland. "How the devil did you manage to get posted back from Northern Ireland?"

"Well, there was only one possible way, so I've taken it. They needed volunteers for Gliding so I offered my services and here I am."

There are no words to express how I felt at this unexpected turn of events. The choice was not mine, it seemed.

"Go on, then, pop in and see your Adjutant and tell him you require a week's leave as you're coming up to Scotland to marry me," Ali was saying. "Remember to tell him that our Banns have already been called."

CHAPTER TWENTY-EIGHT

THE DEED IS DONE

It was wrong, I knew that, I had always known that, but there was his ring on my finger and his photograph always on my desk. I was young and there seemed to be no way out, how could I possibly change my mind again?

"What about my wedding dress?" I asked, to be made even more unsure of myself by his nonchalant reply.

"Oh, I'm afraid we won't be able to manage anything on that scale," he said, as if we were merely discussing the weather. "I'm afraid it will have to be in your uniform."

Even now, after all these years, I still have no recollection of the exact place of his new posting. As in the past, when I was subjected to great moments of elation or despair, I became a zombie, just going through the motions. Naturally, believing themselves to be *au fait* with the real situation, my Officers and small staff swung straight away into action and appeared to be quite excited. As for me, all I can say is that it is absolutely true when I say I have no memory of my long journey back to Scotland, nor do I remember telephoning the WAAF Corporals in room 20, Castle Kennedy.

How different it would have been had I been travelling up to make my marriage vows to James. He would not have hustled me and I would most certainly have been allowed to wear my wedding gown. There would have been no untimely rush, just peace and love and tranquillity. I just supposed he had decided that he was not the marrying kind after all. What I had done — was doing — to poor "Q" far away in India, never crossed my mind.

My long journey left me lethargic, I did not seem to come to life until I arrived, feeling crumpled and very tired. Alan was as gorgeous to look at as ever, with his sunny grin showing his beautiful white teeth, and then I saw a couple of the Corporals too. I was surprised to find Mary Mac had married her Robert and so had a different surname. All this I discovered outside Stranraer Parish Church.

156

The ceremony was equally as vague, just we few and the Reverend in readiness to perform the service. The date was 16th October, 1944, the service was short and soon over, and I noticed Mary's new name as she signed the register, followed by Betty, our little Yiddisher Momma. As we walked out it seemed that the last few flickers of sunlight ebbed away from the day and it was as if the mist seemed in a hurry to pull a veil over the whole scene. The girls had kindly remembered to bring me some bronze chrysanthemums and Mary Mac gave me a small book of household hints. I smiled when I saw that, even as a Clerk/General Duties she had spelt both our Christian names incorrectly, adding the warning "not to use any of the hints within". Strangely enough, I still have that little book today and have used it frequently over the years.

As for the flowers, many, many years were to pass before a complete stranger told me of my latent talent, and it was much later in life, when I became a natural "Character Reader" I discovered that bronze chrysanthemums mean "slighted love".

I still did not know from whence Alan had arrived, but it seems he had taken care of the arrangements from then on and we were soon on a train to Dumfries, waving to my Corporals for the last time, as I never saw any of them again. My mind would not function and I seemed to see everything as if through a haze. My first clear and lasting memory was of placing the flowers in a hand basin in the corner of our bedroom. As I was about to put water in the basin there was a knock on the door and a member of the hotel staff came and took them away to put in a vase. She had that silly look that people have when they guess they have a newly-married couple among them. I cannot even remember what we had for dinner, which sounds stupid when one remembers the many times I had shared hotel meals with Alan, and it was a far cry from that young girl whose speed at learning and retention of memory had brought me thus far.

If we spoke I have no recollection of what we said. I was so very tired and longed to fall into bed and sleep the proverbial hundred years. Not one photograph was taken of us on that day, which was strange when one remembers all the photos and snapshots which we had taken in the past, and our first night together was equally unworthy of being recorded. He held me very gently in a light embrace, more like a brother than a lover. I had never undressed in front of any male since my childhood and cannot recall whether we had the luxury of a bathroom or not. He made no demands on me for which I was deeply grateful, but I was aware of the strange feeling of having the warmth of another body lying beside me.

We had arrived in total darkness and left as soon as we had

breakfasted and packed — no wonder then, that when I returned with a coach party, many many years later, I wandered around Dumfries alone and not one hotel there evoked even a glimmer of recognition.

More refreshed after my sleep, I could at last feel the numbness of both mind and body leaving me, even so, I found it incredible that we were to travel to Suffolk and the home of Alan's parents.

"Are you sure that they are expecting us," I enquired, "and, more to the point, will I be welcome there?"

I had never eaten a full meal on a train before so this new experience was one I can recall.

We were expected but, being late October, it was dark when we arrived and though the drawing room was well furnished and cosy we tended to drift to the large farm kitchen, more on a heat-saving basis, I suspected. His mother was Irish and had a Christian name made famous by a well-known film, but she preferred another name so I was told to use that. Alan was the eldest of their three sons. The middle son was away at Univeristy, whilst the youngest son was quite a bit younger, about seven I would think. He attended a private school where he boarded weekly, so I didn't get to meet him until the weekend. He was a very precocious child and, loving the usage of words myself, I was amused to hear him tell his mother that the Sunday joint of lamb, or rather his portion of it, was very succulent. I must just add here, because I still cringe when it comes to mind, my terrible feeling of inadequacy when Alan's father asked how the word "thwarted" was spelt — I knew it so well, but fell flat on my face because I could not understand his Liverpool accent.

Bedtime arrived and we were wished "Good night" then, as if an afterthought, my new mother-in-law said to Alan "I've put you in your old room, the one you share with Michael." I was normal enough to expect our marriage to take off that night, but was staggered to find we had twin beds several feet apart; no effort having been made to push them together. But worse, much worse, was to follow. I walked along the landing toward the bathroom and was just about to enter it when I was terrified at the sight I could see through the open door of his parents' bedroom. I had noticed that his father limped slightly when he walked, but here I stood, looking at his artificial leg complete with sock and shoe on it, lying on a trunk just inside the door. I decided to be brave and say nothing, pretend I hadn't noticed it, so I slipped into the bathroom and then returned to our bedroom feeling as fresh and scented as any bride should be. But that was the night the elusive piece of jigsaw fell into place.

CHAPTER TWENTY-NINE

PURE FOLLY

All those people who had tried so hard to stop me learning the truth had not been brave enough to shatter the dreams and hopes of a naive, young WAAF, because it was an age when sexual deviations were never mentioned, let alone discussed. I cannot pretend that I blacked out when I saw what was happening on my return, I only wish I could. Neither did I fully comprehend what I was witnessing.

"Alan," I said, "for goodness sake, what do you think you are doing?"

The scales fell from my eyes when he replied. "You don't want to have a baby straight away, do you?"

I forced myself to look at the semen he had just masturbated into a tin mug, before I replied. "I certainly have no thoughts along those lines, but surely we could use some form of protection?" I sat down beside him on his bed, mine still feet away across the room, and I still had not taken in the reason for his strange, and to me abhorrent, act, nor why he had done it. "Why are you so obsessed by sex all of a sudden?" I asked. "It is only a little while since you sent me a book by Marie Stopes with all sorts of remarks in the columns, then another one called *'Having a Baby Easily'* — why did you do that?" How right Barbara had been when she had made the comment on my unworldliness, for even now I still had not reasoned out that it was all a blind to make me unaware that our sexual life would never be normal. As I got into my own bed I began to see it all, or at least to my way of thinking it all fitted.

The reason for his being grounded, maybe? The sudden haste from all sides, the glumness of Rocky and their lack of warmth to Alan when we joined him and his wife? Then there was his parents' hasty appearance on the scene, my own WAAF Commanding Officer, followed by the RAF Commanding Officer. They must have known something that I didn't. Until that moment I had been lucky in my choice of male companions — not one of them had made sexual advances toward me, so that when Alan treated me similarly I took it as being right and proper. I saw now why they had made a last desperate attempt by posting Alan to Northern Ireland with only one more calling of our Banns of Marriage to be made. If just one of them had been brave enough to have spoken about the reason for their interference, I would have listened and responded. But who could blame them in the end, for by posting him to Ireland they had at least called a halt to our marriage — none of us could have foreseen that he would find some way to get back to Scotland and in turn to me.

I could at last begin to understand why so much interference had prevailed from the moment we had announced our intention to marry. Over forty years ago all those people had cared more about me than Alan, even his parents had travelled all that long journey to try to stop their eldest son from marrying a twenty-two-year-old WAAF, yet had failed to put across to her that there was a sexual world of which she knew nothing.

I slept in my own bed for the time we stayed with his parents. Nothing was said so I went through each day and night totally shattered, whilst at the same time still naive enough to believe that Alan might change within a short space of time, but of course, he never did.

Apart from all this, the farm food was wonderful. We had great bowls of porridge or cornflakes with lashings of thick cream, but even this bonus brought me the discomfiture of constipation to contend with. There were two German POWs who helped outside on the farm and when a cow gave birth during our stay the little calf had the dubious honour of being christened "Eileen".

It was not all sadness — far from it. We were taken to meet a few neighbours and once I was taken to watch the bacon being smoked. One small fact sticks in my memory and has, in a strange way, affected my life over the years. One day Alan's mother asked me if I would like to go with her and when I enquired where, I was surprised when she made no secret of the fact that she had won a good sum of money on horse racing.

"Eileen, you should never take from life unless you are prepared to put something back," she remarked. Looking back from this great distance in time, I can see that being Irish she would be attracted to the sport and her logic would make sense. I went with her to a nearby church where she left some of her winnings and I've always remembered that occasion and try to live by her words and have, when possible, put them into practice.

Alan and I were taken by car to the nearest railway station and his mother's parting remark did not surprise me. "Well, I suppose you can always get a divorce!''

We had only been married a week.

We travelled back through Cambridge but I have no memory of which college Alan had probably been sent down from before he joined the RAF. I was taken on a lengthy journey which ended in the Midlands, where I was taken to meet Alan's namesake. The visit was a total disaster as far as I was concerned. The other Alan lived alone in a huge Victorian house. I sensed that he resented my being present and even more so as Ali's wife, without quite knowing why. I sat there mute, not a bit like the bright young WAAF Corporal who had done so much, been to so many places and been in such varied situations, until I was chosen to be the one to help Alan on the Project.

Here I was suffering acute uneasiness and total inferiority. I never saw that Alan again, yet he was to crop up again in correspondence with the passing of time.

Naturally I believed that, now our marriage was a fact, there would be no further interest shown and certainly was unprepared for further action to be taken. There is no disputing that some of the blame was mine — but how could they, the powers that be, see that I would act so totally out of character in their estimation, whilst by my own moral standards I was doing the honourable thing by not playing around?

There was a deeper conviction than that. Looking back over nearly four years I was making my judgement on the assumption that Alan was on a par with the three men, James, Stanley and "Q", none of whom had tried to pressure me into premarital sex. I still had no reason therefore, to think that there would be other complications.

I never learned from any quarter what exactly was known about Alan and his lifestyle before I met him, but the ugly old suspicion reared its head once more as I asked myself why this young, fully-trained pilot, on whom so much had been spent to train him, had been grounded to do a project with me which could so easily have been done by an Officer on the Ground Staff. Well now I only knew the relationship between Alan and me, but I am sure that if the subject had not been skirted around I would have heeded the proffered advice. I think we must both have returned to our respective stations, but I am not sure, I only know that within days I was back with Alan again on Compassionate Leave as he too was being posted to India.

I like to think that it was not just because Alan had slipped through the net, but that they deeply regretted that they had not given me that oh! so very personal warning and were giving me the chance to continue the life and work I loved so much. It was obvious now that we were all aware that they realised their mistake in sending him across to Ireland — he should have been posted straight away to India, and time and distance would surely have averted this terrible mistake.

I remember taking Alan to the home of my now eldest sister and how surprised I was that she was able to rustle up some really wonderful cooking, both then and again when the Assistant Adjutant gave Sergeant Rex from the Station W/O's Office a lift as we all travelled South one weekend and they called in to have tea and to pick me up on the way back — the car was badly scraped that night when another car sped past us too close in total darkness. I recall the remarks made by my sister concerning Alan and I and guessed she would not have accepted the fact that our marriage was a sham and had never been consummated. I wished I had not been so naive as I could have had it annulled even before he came back.

It was when I finally got round to taking Alan to "Orchard Cottage" that the full impact of the mistake I had made really hit home.

Olive caught me alone for a short period and spoke to me in her forthright manner. "I'm sorry to have to tell you, Eileen, but I don't like this man you have married."

I understood her but made no comment, merely reminding her that by Bonfire Night he would have left for India and our three-week marriage would be over until the war came to an end. I dreaded that she might tell me that she no longer wished me to continue my weekends at the cottage, or even meet her on my days off for lunch together in The Cadena in Oxford, but I think she realised that we now needed each other for very different reasons.

"I will see you again real soon then, Eileen, just like before" she said as we left and I was comforted by her words. I nodded as I held back my tears, unable to speak.

Alan opened up an account with one of the five major banks, and arranged that one pound per day, or to be precise, £30.00 per month was to be credited into it — a lot of money in those days — and then he was gone. If only . . . are words of regret, and I knew my "if only" was "If only they had posted Alan to India before we married, even with our Banns of Marriage called, we would have been distanced long enough to have realised that a marriage between us was an act of pure folly."

Right to the end Alan left me in despair, for try as I might to make him understand that there is a correct time for ending even

Compassionate Leave, all he would say was "You are an Officer's wife now."

"Alan," I said, "I know you regard my Corporal status as being unimportant, to you it is just the lowest rank one can hold as a Non-Commissioned Officer, but to me mine is very special."

I still arrived back, one day AWOL, and fraught with tension. Of course, they had every right to put me on a charge. Remember no one knew of the background to our marriage, so although I received only the mildest of verbal reprimands, I knew it was on the grounds of their sympathy toward me having been so newly married, only to have my new husband posted to India. I like to think that my being in charge of the Orderly Room, with a hitherto unblemished record, also held me in good stead.

CHAPTER THIRTY

CINDERELLA AND PRINCE CHARMING

It was clear from that day onward that I intended to settle back into my normal routine. I told no one about my sham marriage, nor did I tell any member of my assorted family. In those days one was not only shy about bringing up such a subject, but there was more than an element of shame that went with it, so I decided to stay silent. My work was my saviour and even those who were brave enough to ask me out for a date were given the cold shoulder. One could say I was off men and not in the least bit sorry.

Nevertheless changes crept in unbidden by me. The first was when I asked the Adjutant if I could pop into the town to cash a cheque.

"How much is the cheque for, Corporal?" he asked.

"I'm afraid it's for £20, Sir," I said.

"Fetch your cheque in, I see we can run to that." When I thanked him he just said quite nonchalantly, as he was returning the box into one of his desk drawers, "Always pop in and see me first" and I don't recall cashing a cheque in any other way. My trips to the bank in "Chippy" became unnecessary after that.

Twice I surprised men who arrived in the Orderly Room. One had just married a girl from Farnham — I had attended school with her sometime during my youth, but I did not recognise her husband, nor he me. It was the address he gave me which gave the game away, well, with regard to his rank, anyway. The second one was the brother of a girl I had been with at an all-girls' school in my latter youth, and I knew him quite well. I was to learn later from this sister that he went home and said to her "You'll never guess who practically runs our station?" He then went on to tell her. "She has done well for herself, stripes and all on her sleeves, yet she just looked up and said 'Hello, Les,' just as if she had seen me the day before!" I was pleased to hear that he added "She's not the least bit stuck up."

All the same I was to post him overseas some months later, and this was well into 1944.

The actual date of the marriage of our Medical Corporal Assistant, Anne, escapes me, yet the event remains vividly in my mind, probably more so than for any of the other guests who attended the wedding. Anne dearly longed for a white wedding but thought the likelihood was hopeless until someone reminded her that the Orderly Room Corporal had never had the chance to wear her white wedding gown, which was still as new, together with all the trimmings — so Anne approached me on the subject. It seemed pointless to refuse, I would never need it now and so I was to end up being very pleased about the outcome.

Anne's mother was "over the moon" when we all arrived. Officers and Other Ranks were all packed tightly into the Station truck and all looking a bit creased when we entered Anne's parents' home somewhere in the Worcester/Malvern area. There was a special hug for me from her mother, who had been on tenterhooks to meet this WAAF who had become the Fairy Godmother and had wrought a miracle for this happy day. When the photographs were taken of the Medical Officer in his uniform, Anne wearing my dress and our WAAF Commanding Officer next to the bride for the sake of etiquette, Anne's mother fussed around making sure that I was next in line. It was a really lovely wedding and I treasure the photograph I was given — the only photo I have of the wedding dress I never wore myself. It still looks lovely and looking back to that unforgettable day, I am truly happy that someone gained some extra happiness from my lending it. In fact I might well have suggested she keep it and I'm fairly sure that that is what happened to it. There is our young, very handsome Assistant Adjutant and many other familiar faces of varying ranks all on that one happy photograph.

It was autumn once more and running down to Christmas 1944. I literally lived the life of a nun. Of course, letters from Alan were arriving from India, and I would type my replies to these when I went back to the Orderly Room at nights. I must confess when doing this I did suffer "guilt pangs" remembering that "Q" was out there too. I never kept his letters, just his photograph on which he proclaimed "With ALL my Love — 'Q' ", but I kept Mac's postcards together with the small, very beautiful studio portrait on which he had written "Lots of Love — Mac" and which he had given me almost as soon as we had met in the spring of 1941 before I had reached my nineteenth birthday. Both of these photographs and both the cards survived the war along with all the cards and silver keys I had received on my twenty-first birthday spent in

M

Cosford Hospital. And now here I was all set to spend my fourth Christmas as a WAAF.

There was, however, to be a small incident which again took place on a day I had kept an appointment and so was late arriving at HQ. It was another charge and I could hardly believe my ears when the facts were given to me.

"What the Hell has a Warrant Officer of his calibre been doing?" I asked, adding thoughtlessly, "Is that the W/O with the lovely brown eyes?" It seems he had breached the fencing which ran up the side of the main road on camp, merely to nick a small spruce for the coming festivities, but this ground was marked "Strictly Private" and was hence out of bounds to all ranks, so the charge went ahead. It was soon old hat. Well, it would have been but for my remark about his eyes. I had not looked to see who was present in the Orderly Room at the time — I always worked with the idea that it was my office, so I just said what I wanted to.

A notice had gone up in various places with regard to a Christmas dance which was being held in the Sergeants' Mess, by invitation only, but this year it was to be different. Could it be a sign of hopefulness, just as the more or less disbanding of Administration had been, that we were being allowed to wear civilian dress on this occasion?

Our WAAF Commanding Officer took me by surprise when she called me into her office opposite the Orderly Room to speak to me. "Please, Corporal, do tell me that you are attending this forthcoming dance and social affair in the Segeants' Mess. I am really quite worried about you. So you are now married, but surely that does not mean that you cannot allow yourself some relaxation? Please think about it if only for my peace of mind."

"I am deeply touched by your concern for my welfare," I smiled as I replied, "but even if I wanted to attend I could not do so, Ma'am, because you have signed the Guardroom rota for that night. You probably did not notice that I am to be Guardroom NCO on that date."

"Well, then, you must find a reliable Leading Aircraftwoman who doesn't like dancing. That is surely an easy enough task for you, and then you can give her the go-ahead, as an NCO, to hold the fort until midnight, when you can dash back before the others and just button everything up in the Guardroom in your own efficient manner." Suddenly we both had the same thought and started to laugh at the idea of my being a real Cinderella in this odd situation.

I only ever rang Olive at the department store in an emergency, but I put through a call to the fur department and told her of my plight.

"Of course you must attend" she replied. "Can you get a night away and come down to 'Orchard Cottage' this week? There must be something of mine that will fit you." I was a bit shattered when she settled for my wearing one of her "little black numbers", all the rage at that time. Some of my puppy fat had fallen away and my eating had suffered during my months of emotional stress, so the dress fitted me perfectly. Olive added the final touch — a real piece of mink wired into the shape of a flower. I knew then that I looked, as the Americans say, like a million dollars, and I felt really grown up at last. I arranged which day I would return it, but more to the point, I knew Olive would want to know every detail of that night.

There was a quiet period in the hut, on the right side a WAAF was snuggled under her blankets, whilst another WAAF on my side but way down near the door at the far end, was the only other person present. Oddly enough both shared the same Christian name, but there the sameness ended. I could always sense when one of the girls wanted to approach me on a personal subject and I was not wrong this time. "J" at the far end approached me to make her request, which in no way surprised me, but her request for my permission to allow her to go down the lane for a little while, did. I just looked at her, puzzled.

"Did you really say that you want to go down the lane?" I asked. "That unmade road leading up to the WAAF site, which we refer to as 'the lane'? Well, of course you can go, but I must admit I am very curious as to your strange request, but you do not have to give me your reason."

"It is in connection with the dance, Corporal," she explained. "Daddy's chauffeur is bringing down a selection of dresses so that I can make my choice." I could hardly believe my ears and I showed my total amazement.

"But 'J', what on earth are you doing being in this hut under my command when surely you could have bought your way in as a Commissioned Officer?"

"Oh, Corporal, you'll never know how lucky I consider myself. You seem to be totally unaware that each WAAF in this hut feels as I do, and we each know that if one of us is ever posted there are many who wish to fill such a vacancy, several times over."

"Go on," I said, completely puzzled.

"Well, take me, for instance. You have my documents to hand, yet it is obvious that you know none of my personal data because you treat each one of us as an entity in our own right. Can you honestly remember when you gave an order to any WAAF in this hut, even though you set such a high standard?"

"Methinks you do me too much honour," I said, joshing her,

"and if I did not know you so well, I might even suggest you are fawning!" Almost immediately an idea sprang to mind. "Please, 'J', sit on my bed," I found myself saying, "I have a request to make of you which may, on the surface at least, appear to make gobbledegook of all you have just said. See the WAAF on the other side of the hut who appears to be sleeping? Well, I am telling you in the strictest confidence that she will not be attending the dance for the simple reason she came from a home to enlist. She hasn't any hope of getting a dress to wear from anywhere. Now, what if I break my second rule, having just broken one, and ask you if there is any chance that among the dresses your chauffeur brings, one of them might fit her, and if so, would you be willing to help me spring a big surprise on her by lending her one for the night, with the promise that you will never let her, or any other member of the hut, know?"

We left the hut together and went down the lane, where the chauffeur got out of the huge car. "J" introduced me as being "My Corporal" and, to my utter amazement, he gave me an unexpected salute. He had five dresses on board and we fiddled around in the back of the car. "J" selected hers first, then spoke to the surprised chauffeur. "Tell Mummy I've taken two, one is a little longer than the other."

"Very good, Miss 'J'," he said and then enquired when he should come to pick them up. I hoped he didn't think the second one was for me!

When we reached the hut I asked "J" to disappear for a short time and when she had gone I went over to the taller "J" and gently shook her, going along with her pretence of being asleep.

"Wake up, sleepy head," I said, "I want you to get up and go and have a bath, here's some nice talc and some shampoo for your hair." She looked at me aghast, how right "J" had been, I was now breaking a third rule, I realised.

"Is that just a request, Corporal," she asked me, "or is it an order? Never in my life have I heard you have to request any WAAF to have a bath. We would not be in your hut unless we were clean by your own high standards."

"I'm sorry," I said, "but, yes, it is an order."

She got up sulkily to obey and returned with her lovely hair wet and curly and it was then that her eyes fell on the dress laid out on her bed.

"Now, 'J', I am not going to say anything, hurry up and dry your locks and try this on for size. It's yours for the evening, no questions asked or answered, understand?"

"Oh, Corporal . . . ," she said, but I reminded her that I too would be a Cinderella on that night as I had to leave just before midnight to be on Guard Duty.

"When you wear it, I know you will take care of it, you need not answer any questions and all you have to do is to return it to me afterwards, when we are alone together." So I broke every rule, bar one, that I had ever made, but there were three happy hearts and sometimes rules are made to be broken.

There was a small sequel to this tiny deception. It happened in London after the war had ended and was very enjoyable, but it does not belong in this book which will only take in my four and a half "passionate years".

I had received an air-mail letter from Alan only that morning and although enclosures were not permitted, I was not the least bit surprised when a snapshot fell to the floor. It was a picture of a young woman much about my own age, dressed in shorts and sprawled out on some grass, reminding me of Portpatrick and the grounds of Castle Kennedy when I had served for nearly a year in Scotland. I have cause to remember that letter because when I read it I found Alan was passing this person off as being a cousin of the other Alan he had taken me to meet, somewhere in the Midlands, I think. More than that, he even went as far as to request my opinion of her. But he was no longer writing to "an innocent abroad", so I quietly swore to myself and tore it to shreds with no intention of making any reference to it at all. I relate this because I think in part, at least, its receipt helped colour my behaviour on that long-past December night in 1944.

There was, however, another event which had occurred a week or so before the Christmas festivities held on the camp. Because we were able to hold our dances and socials on Christmas Eve, Christmas Night or Boxing Day, the ones in the local town tended to be held a week or so earlier to make sure of a good attendance.

I cannot remember who coaxed me to attend with them — it was another WAAF, but that is all I recall. I must have worried lest she found herself a partner who would escort her back to camp, but it didn't work out that way at all. When we arrived it seemed as if we might be in for a dull evening, when, much to our surprise, a few Officers from our camp drifted in and from then on the dance really took off. Our unexpected fun was short-lived for just as I was getting along well dancing with a Canadian pilot named Bill, the air-raid siren sounded. I was shattered because I could not recall the last time I had heard the wail of a siren. However, Bill was quick thinking and turned back and grabbed my greatcoat before taking my hand and rushing with me from the dance hall.

It was a very dark night and I had no idea where we were so I asked him where he was taking me.

"To the shelter, of course, where else?" I was even more amazed when he took me unerringly to one fairly close by and then found that he and I were the only occupants in that damp, dark shelter.

"How on earth did you know where this shelter was?" I asked.

"Oh, I always make sure about things like that!" he replied.

"Does that indicate that you have attended dances in the town before tonight, then?" I asked.

"Only once," he told me, "but I was not lucky last time."

Puzzled by that I asked what exactly his comment implied, and was both surprised and flattered by his reply.

"It is a well-known fact that the Orderly Room Corporal does very little socialising and I could hardly believe my eyes or my luck when I entered and saw you in the hall."

"But I don't know you, so why the interest?"

"You will think me totally stupid," he said, "but the truth is that from the first time I ever saw you I wanted to get to know you. I was shattered to find you are married because I also fell in love with you on sight."

"Yes," I said, "I was married for about three weeks last October — my husband is now serving in India, hence my almost total nonexistent social life."

"Well, just for tonight I'll be 'just your Bill' and you can be 'just my Eileen'." And so we shared some time in that dark, damp shelter.

"Have you heard the saying 'Never go out with the Orderly Room Corporal, or you will be sure to end up with a stinking cold'?" I asked him and he laughed.

"Is that so?" he asked.

"They say it's because I accept only a few dates and then I keep my men sitting on the grass too long."

He walked me back to camp, another perfect gentleman. "Please, Eileen, may I kiss you good night?" he asked and a strong feeling of *déjà vu* assailed me.

"Not until you let me tell you something," I found myself saying. He waited whilst I struggled to find the right words, words that would not hurt him. "Within weeks of my enlisting I met and fell in love with a Scotsman who was known as Mac. I did not realise how deeply I loved him — and yes, I would have married him had he asked me, to save you asking that question. Then this evening you walked into my life and ever since something has been teasing my mind and only now have I suddenly realised what that something is. Forgive me, Bill, please? But you are so very much like him — it is as if my world has turned full circle. You are an almost perfect match for him — the same height and your hair and eyes are also a perfect match. He was gentle and quiet like you.'' I desperately wanted him to kiss me so I simply said ''So now do you still want to kiss me?''

''I not only want to kiss you but I am certain that had you been free I would ask you here and now to marry me! No, you haven't hurt me, quite the reverse in fact — I feel honoured that for just a tiny moment in our lives I have met up to someone you obviously loved very dearly. We had this short time together tonight and I feel certain that neither of us will ever forget it.''

He held me lightly in his arms and leaned forward and kissed me — he wasn't my Mac but the closest I ever came to being in love with his image.

All this was behind me on the night I saw my chosen LACW take her place in the Guardroom and acquainted her with the fact that, like Cinderella, I'd be back at midnight to take over the final duties for the night. I walked alone down the lane — there were no strange men hanging around of whom one might be afraid in those days.

My entrance into the Mess where the dance was being held remains etched in my memory. There was only a sprinkling of dancers on the floor, whilst many of the other WAAFs were dressed in gaily-printed cotton dresses and sitting together like wallflowers.

My mind was wrestling with the fact that in Olive's ''little black number'' with its mink flower as its only embellishment, I was very definitely the odd one out. How quickly a situation can change, especially when one is as VIP as I always seemed to be. I heard a murmur among the girls.

''Oh! Look at Corporal! Doesn't she look a million dollars in that dress and with her lovely hair swept up?'' This was to prove to be only the beginning.

It seemed that in no time at all we were inundated by Aircrew members and amongst them was Bill. He wasted no time in coming over to ask me to dance — that at least was something all his own, because Mac did not dance. At least, it would be more true to say that we both expected it to be something all his own, until four other pilots decided they too wanted to dance with me. Bill was so obviously disappointed, and so for that matter was I.

''It's only because I'm married and hold a prominent post,'' I said to him. ''They feel safe with me, no ties, no commitments afterwards.'' It was quite the loveliest night I've ever had at a dance. I was being constantly passed from one to the other in rapid succession. We didn't even stop to drink, a mere orangeade had to suffice. I had high hopes that as the evening progressed some of them would let up, but no, they kept up the momentum till the end.

"Eileen, please let me be the one who walks you up the lane?" Bill managed to ask, but I had to explain that I was committed to leaving about ten minutes to midnight as I genuinely was "Guardroom Corporal" and had promised my WAAF Commanding Officer that I would not let her down. So there was no second kiss, just a hurried few words as we said "Good night".

I kept my word and as I walked back alone I mused on the oddities of life. Only a short while before I had been a humble Corporal saluted by a chauffeur, now here I was returning in my borrowed black dress, which I now knew had been eye-catching because it was like no other worn by any other WAAF.

It was a few days later when we were all back to normal that I received a telephone call from Anne, the Corporal in Medical Quarters, who had worn my white wedding gown. I was shocked by her words.

"What kind of bitch are you, anyway? I know it's a standing joke that men have only to take you out and they catch a cold, but you might at least have sent Bill some kind of note or message for me to pass on to him!"

"I've neither seen nor heard anything about Bill since the night of the dance. I truly don't have the least idea what you are talking about."

"Oh, sorry," she said, immediately contrite, "I forgot you don't deal with Officers' documentation. Bill is in here with double pneumonia. I should have let you know sooner because now it's too late — he is quite ill and so is being moved to hospital." Still she could not stop herself quipping, "You certainly did a good job on him," but was then serious again. "Yes, of course, I'll pass on a verbal message before he leaves. It's true, isn't it Eileen, that you were both very attracted to each other?" I could not deny it so I told her that it was true and that no one would regret his going more than I and that I should never see him again — though, I added, it was no doubt for the best. I was remembering how my Mac must have fallen in love with me instantly, just as Bill had done!

I've never forgotten his surname nor the hint of a long-lost love he had brought into my life. But this was not to be the final tragedy of my life, as I was to find out too late . . . . .

CHAPTER THIRTY-ONE

LOOSE ENDS

And so it was January once more — January 1945. There probably had been a New Year's Dance and if I did attend I would have thought of it as being "Hogmanay" and wondered if Mac had gone to share it with his mother at his home in Hollybush, Ayr. There was the inevitable snow but it was not sufficient to stop us riding our cycles. I have good reason to remember that.

One morning an Aircrew Warrant Officer presented himself in the Orderly Room and announced that he was "attached". His name was Warrant Officer Davidson. His documents were in my "In" tray, so I was expecting him but I had him down as being "posted" and told him so.

"What difference does it make, anyway, Corporal?" he asked, but I think he knew damned fine what the difference was. I patiently explained that if one was "attached" it would only be necessary to sign on as being on Strength at HQ and at the appropriate Mess to enable one to get meals. Finally, he would sign on at the Police Section to allow access to and from camp.

"And if posted?" he asked and I told him that it would be necessary to sign on in all sections on camp, such as Armoury, Flying Control, Link Trainer; in other words a full sign on job.

He said "Well, then I am attached."

I never argued with him, I simply lifted the telephone and asked to be put through to our Main Station Orderly Room. Rarely a day passed when I did not have some reason to call them, so I was quite well known. I told the male Sergeant about the situation and he just laughed.

"I don't rate his chances very high — hold on a tick, I'll check for you." He came back on laughing and said "Yes, he is definitely posted."

"If I hold out the telephone will you shout down it, please?" I said, jokingly. "He doesn't seem to want to believe me."

173

I offered Warrant Officer Davidson the appropriate form to take round to all the sections to get signed on.

"When you arrived Corporal, did you have to sign on in every section?" he asked, much to my amazement. "If so, how did you do it?"

He was beginning to irk me but I kept my cool. "I hardly think that is any of your business but I do have a 'Runner' and he probably did it for me. If not then I would have cycled round."

"Oh! Then perhaps I could borrow your cycle?" he enquired.

"Certainly not, for two reasons — I shall need it quite soon to cycle to lunch," I said. "If I loaned my cycle to everyone, I would hardly ever have the use of it myself."

I did not think any more about this incident, though I did hear down the grapevine that that same Warrant Officer had fallen foul of the Station Adjutant, but I did not learn the reason for this, nor did it interest me.

New rules were still being brought out even at this late stage of the war and one of these was because the Cookhouse had put in a complaint that far too many Aircrew Members were putting in for "Night Flying" Suppers. So it came about that Flying Control were to telephone the exact number flying each night to the Orderly Room, who in turn would let the Cookhouse know. It was still very cold weather-wise but most of the snow had disappeared when I answered my telephone one morning.

"The Orderly Room, who's calling?"

"This is the Warrant Officer with the lovely brown eyes."

I was absolutely flabbergasted. "Who told you that?" I asked and he laughed.

"You should be more careful when you make remarks like that, even if you did make it in the Orderly Room. I'll tell you the number of Night Flying Suppers if you promise to come out with me tonight, and I'll also tell you who was eavesdropping."

He was a really nice fellow so I did not need much persuading.

I think we went into the local town cinema but my memory of that night picks up from when we had walked back to Camp. Nick said "I'm hungry, aren't you?" I was, but there was no Mess open and our ranks were different too, but he soon solved the problem. "I've got some plain chocolate in my sleeping quarters, shall we go and get that?"

"Oh! no, we can't do that. What if I get caught in your part of the camp?"

"You're afraid to come, aren't you — afraid I have designs on you. Well, let me tell you something. If I did not have my 'anchor' at home to whom I am engaged, I might think it well worth a try, and you are married anyway, so come on, let's go!''

Where the snow had lain it was now almost a quagmire as we squelched our way across the field. He opened the door of the hut and hastened me inside because of blackout regulations. He really did have some chocolate and so we sat on his bed and ate that. I noticed there was another bed in the hut already made up and with some striped pyjamas on it.

"Who shares the hut with you, Nick?" I asked and he laughed.

"You might well remember him, I believe he gave you a hard time when he tried to be 'attached' instead of being posted. He's due back tonight from some leave and I've been playing 'Mother' and made his bed up for him." He went on roguishly to tell me that it would be easy to make love with me there, but he just might return and catch us. I knew he was teasing so I listened while he filled me in on his "Anchor" back home. He then walked me back to WAAF Quarters and as far as I was concerned it had been just a very enjoyable evening, not to be repeated, since we were both tied up.

But there was a sequel, albeit a small one. I was very surprised when I picked up my telephone to hear Nick on the line.

"You're too late," I said. "Someone has already rung about the Night Flying Suppers."

"Yes, I know," he said, "but I think I owe you this one for 'my lovely brown eyes'. Remember we talked about Davidson the other night? Well, I have news for you. He'll be taking the WAAF Church Parade on Sunday and has told me that he intends to march you into the ground."

"You really are a lovely man," I said, "but here's one WAAF Corporal who won't be on parade."

"You mean you can get let off?" he asked me and I told him that it was well within my scope. "Thanks a lot for letting me know and watch what happens."

I immediately stuck a small piece of paper into the typewriter and typed myself out a "chit". I knew it would be useless to apply to the WAAF Commanding Officer so I typed "The above-mentioned Corporal is unable to attend Church Parade on (here I filled in the date) owing to pressure of work in the Orderly Room." I then drew a line, ending it with ADJUTANT and took it along to his office.

"Sir," I said, "I wonder if you would be kind enough to sign this chit for me, as I particularly want to miss parade on Sunday."

"Boyfriend trouble, Corporal?" he asked and I said "Well, you could say that."

"Who is taking the Parade on Sunday?" he asked and when I said "Davidson" he laughed and stretched out his hand.

"Oh, give it here, if it's Davidson, I'll sign it twice!" This showed yet another way the system worked.

I lived my war, I rarely read the newspapers to see how it was going — I was far too busy for that. I did listen in, but only during periods of great importance or when the weather made it impossible to leave my Billet. Nevertheless, I was aware that the war in Europe was coming to an end and as the weeks ran down toward early May, 1945, it was obvious that preparations were being made with regard to winding down members of staff. I realised that Satellites might well be the first to be closed right down. I had started out with nearly four months to go to my nineteenth birthday, an absolute nobody, the lowest trade, the lowest grade and the lowest paid. Now I was well into my twenty-third year. My greatest pride was the fact that I had been given two small Orderly Rooms to run successively and, of lesser importance, that I had earned my Non-Commissioned status. Yet, looking back, I realise that my rank must have meant more to me than I had supposed, for it was chiefly the cause of my making the greatest mistake of my life.

The Adjutant called me in to point out that, as a married woman, I would be one of the first to be demobilised. Perhaps, if he had worded his appeal differently, I might not have reacted quite so strongly. On the other hand there is the old song which goes "If we'd thought a bit about the end of it", which I certainly had not done!

"Please, Corporal, do stay on? We cannot wind this place down without you, I could get you your third stripe tomorrow — there's surely no need for you to rush back to Civvy Street. Your husband is still in India and you don't have children to consider."

It was the possibility of a third stripe which roused my reply. "Well, I can't see the point of becoming a Sergeant and then watch the station fall apart around me. I don't think I could stay to work without the bustle." So I made my decision to leave when my time came.

At last V-E Day came, 8th May, 1945. We were called to muster at eleven a.m. to be informed that the war in Europe was over. Our Commanding Officer had seemingly begun his private celebrations a bit earlier for I remember how he swayed slightly on his feet as he made the announcement. We were told that we were free for the rest of that day.

Now that the actual day had arrived I started to have the "Jitters" as to what would happen to me when I was no longer part of the only life I had known and loved for so long. A group had got together with their cycles and suggested I got mine and joined them. There was a nice little pub our side of town which would be popular on that sunny morning as it had a very pleasant garden. Here we stretched ourselves out on the grass under the trees and I imagine we were all full of mixed emotions: wonderment, elation, memories, yet all would be tinged by the sadness of our pending disbandment. As I dozed lightly I pondered about all the trestle tables being erected in the streets of London and all the other big cities, and even in the tiny hamlets, where the children would attend their parties. There would be flag waving and bunting and some children too young to understand any of it! Yet here we just lay and supped our drink.

Someone had bought me a pint mug of cider and left me to my reveries and before I knew what was happening there followed a second and then a third. I kept recalling *"Cider with Rosie"* by Laurie Lee and then I felt a tear roll down my face because my sister, Rosalie, was known as Rosie and she had died when I was seventeen and a half. I was getting maudlin by the time the fourth mug of cider was placed beside me. The sun was making me drowsy. Drinking had never been a pastime of mine and only in moderation, mostly at dances and socials.

I was still quietly musing when I became aware of the stir among my companions and heard them urging me to hurry as we ought to be getting back for lunch. Looking back, I wonder if I was trying to blot out, not the past, but the uncertain future which lay ahead of me. For whatever reason I allowed myself to drink to excess. I remain equally puzzled by my achievement of returning to camp on my cycle, which upon arrival, I promptly mislaid.

By today's jargon I was as "pissed as a newt" yet much of the day's happenings remain in my memory. By mislaying my cycle I had no irons (cutlery), as they were in my saddlebag. As I floundered around the camp I was slightly aware of people saying "Gosh, look at the Orderly Room Corporal. Who would have thought of seeing her like that?" I remember reaching the Sergeants' Mess but somehow I was having difficulty in steering myself up the concrete path and so ended up trampling all over the flowerbeds.

The windows were open to the May sunshine and Davidson happened to be standing near one looking out.

"Please could you lend me your irons? I've mislaid my cycle and they are in the saddlebag," I asked him. He fetched me some, by which time many of the Warrant Officers and Flight Sergeants had come to see the spectacle I was making of myself. Among them was Nick and he seemed to take over.

"We ought to get her to the Other Ranks' Mess to eat some

lunch," he said to Dave, "and then see that she gets back to her hut on the WAAF site." Then everything changed — Rosa my Clerk/Typist happened to be passing and Nick asked her to take over and follow the same instructions. As we were about to leave I heard Nick tell Rosa that there were to be celebrations held in the Sergeants' Mess that afternoon and I promptly announced that I wanted to attend. Rosa said something about seeing how I was after I'd had a sleep.

When Rosa came later I was almost sobered up and was able to get dressed in my best blues and go with her. The only thing that could be said in my favour that afternoon was that I was at least quiet as I crept from lap to lap professing my love to each individual. I heard Nick say to Rosa that he would ring "The White Hart" hotel in Chipping Norton to see if they could fit the four of us in for dinner that evening, though doubtless they would be inundated on this, of all nights. He was successful in securing a table for the four of us, so doubtless we would recall in the future where we spent the evening of V-E Day and I can even remember that we enjoyed a lovely meal of roast lamb, with mint sauce and all the trimmings, all at the expense of the two Warrant Officers. I had imagined that I was with Nick and Rosa with Dave, but in the end it did not seem to matter much either way.

Gradually the staff was getting more and more depleted, but I had another three months more there before my Demobilisation Order came through. I was to be demobbed at RAF Witham, near Birmingham, on the 13th August, 1945 — just eleven days before my twenty-third birthday. Of course, I did complete my full four and a half years for we were on paid recall leave for two months — just in case the war flared up again — so I was officially on strength until 8th October, 1945. I was paid for 1,377 days, plus my NCO entitlement. I was very proud when I received my RAF Service and Release Book and found I had been awarded two "Superiors" — the first for my service, the second for my ability as an NCO. "Superior" was the highest grade obtainable except for the rare Excellent given only for very outstanding proficiency. Likewise, my character grade, which again was the highest, being VG. My reference reads "Capable and conscientious, would make an excellent secretary, a pleasant personality."

I had started with the lowest trade, the lowest grade and the lowest paid but had lifted myself in five short weeks from the Cookhouse to working in HQ and to finally end up running my own two Orderly Rooms.

But now my four and a half "Passionate Years" had come to an end and I was lying in my bed in the farmhouse in Suffolk when Alan's mother brought me my breakfast and a newspaper which proclaimed "V-J Day" — Victory over the Japanese. Ahead of me stretched my new life, a life with so many loose strings to be tied — or untied — and so much uncertainty. A life of which I stood in awe as I agonized over my future and what it held in store for me. I was to wish, often, that I had accepted my third stripe and my chance to stay on as a WAAF Sergeant, at least for another six months.

But if wishes were horses, beggars would ride — I was a civilian once more . . . . .

APPENDAGE . . . . .

APPENDAGE

I went back to Farnham to work for almost two years, silently trapped in my sham marriage — because Alan took that long to return by sea with his Wren Officer, instead of flying back to release me from his selfish act of tying me down in a three-week pointless marriage, because he had known the reason all along.

I have passed lightly over my meeting in the Midlands with someone from home. I cannot even recall how this meeting had come into being. He gave me no indication that the occasion was in any way special to him, nor did he write to me after it. So I did not tell him that he had given me my very first kiss when I was about fourteen years old, nor about the schoolgirl crush I had on him which was often the cause of my going the long way home from school, just to pass his house. If only he had given me the merest hint!

It did not matter until the day his sister introduced me as "This is Eileen, we had high hopes at one time that she would become my sister-in-law." I was totally shattered.

I saw him one evening, standing all alone at the bar in "The Blue Boy" — I stayed there until I was fortunate enough to get digs in "The Fairfield" and was passing through to go to my room. I could not explain; we did not speak, I went up and wept on my bed.

Just seeing him again made me wish that I too could have returned to my home town, as many who had left to enlist like me had done and, like them, I could have settled happily back in Farnham.

But from then on it was a case of 'Send in the Clowns'.